MW01286644

The Book

HUSKER SPORTS TRIVIA
Copyright © 1995 by ExHusker Press a division of Cross Training
Publishing

Library of Congress Cataloging-in-Publication Data

Greunke, Lowell
Lowell Greunke

Husker Sports Trivia / Lowell Greunke
Published by ExHusker Press a division of Cross Training
Publishing, Grand Island, Nebraska 68803
Distributed in the United States and Canada by Cross Training
Publishing

No part of this book may be reproduced without written permission except for brief quotation in books and critical reviews. For information write Cross Training Publishing, P.O. Box 1541, Grand Island, Nebraska 68802.

Printed in the United States of America

ISBN 1-887002-29-4

9015 "F" Street, Omaha, Nebraska 68127-1397
Phone: (402) 592-0000 • Fax (402) 592-8323

ExHusker Press
a Division of
Cross Training Publishing
P.O. Box 1541
Grand Island, NE 68802
(308) 384-5762
ExHusker Press is owned and operated by Gordon Thiessen,
an ex-Husker, who played defensive end from 1975-80.

Dedication

This book is dedicated to Tom Osborne. Like the State of Nebraska, Coach Osborne continues to confound the nation by valuing substance over hype, integrity over popularity, the right way over the easy way. Tom Osborne is a great coach but he is a greater man and a symbol of the core values that Nebraskans hold dear.

Introduction

Husker Sports Trivia, the book, was written as a companion product for the board game, Husker Sports Trivia™. The authors are well aware that there are many fans of University of Nebraska athletics who do not care to play board games but still enjoy testing their knowledge of Husker sports. This book will enable those fans to quiz themselves on the same questions as those used in the board game without having to find other fans to play a game. The first section of the book contains questions that are relatively easy to answer. The second, and larger, portion of the book presents trivia questions that will test even the most experienced and knowledgeable Husker fan. Both sections contain a large percentage of questions on Husker football but also test a fan's knowledge of other University of Nebraska sports. Both men's and women's athletic programs are included.

A sense of euphoria and vindication was felt by Husker fans everywhere on New Year's Day, 1995 when Tom Osborne's team finally claimed that elusive national championship. The year 1995 has been one of celebration of Husker athletics. This trivia book in meant to continue that positive feeling. You will find no questions and answers here that will bash or criticize the University of Nebraska and its athletics programs. The national media and our opponents seem to concentrate on that aspect already. The authors will not participate in such negativity. *Husker Sports Trivia* has been written to praise the accomplishments of Husker athletics and to encourage fans to relive glory days and enjoyable memories that those teams have provided.

Do you think you know all there is to know about Husker athletics? Take the challenge. Find out just how much you really do know. At the very least it should be an enjoyable journey. Hopefully, you will also learn some new bits of Husker lore that you can use to stump your friends and family. Have a good time!

Go Big Red!

TABLE OF CONTENTS

University of Nebraska
Bob Devaney

I was happy to be asked to write the foreword for this book that compliments the Husker Sports Trivia™ board game. The history of the University of Nebraska and its athletic programs are both diverse and exciting.

I've enjoyed reminiscing the numerous historical moments of my 30 plus year association with the Cornhuskers. The facts contained in this book have brought back many wonderful memories. There are facts in this book that made me chuckle and some that have surprised even me. Every Husker fan should indeed learn from and enjoy this book so they too can become a Husker Sports Trivia expert.

Robert Devaney

1. Athletes

47 Q: Who scored the winning touchdown in the 1971 Nebraska/Oklahoma game?

1 Q: Who was the Heisman Trophy winner in 1972?

2 Q: Who won both the Outland Trophy and the Lombardi Award in1972?

3 Q: What NU running back led the nation in rushing in 1983?

4 Q: Who was awarded the Heisman Trophy in 1983?

5 Q: Who was the back-to-back Outland Trophy winner in 1981 and 1982?

6 Q In spite of his deaf condition, what NU defensive tackle played in the NFL for the Denver Broncos?

7 Q: Who was the MVP of the 1995 Orange Bowl?

8 Q: What NU basketball player was the MVP of the Big Eight tournament in 1994?

9 Q: What two running backs each gained over 1000 yards during the 1992 season?

10 Q: What Husker running back earned the nickname "Marvelous"?

11 Q: What was the jersey number of Heisman Trophy winner Johnny Rodgers?

12 Q: What NU running back holds an NCAA rushing record with 7.16 yards per carry for his career?

13 Q: Which Omaha high school produced Husker great Johnny Rodgers?

14 Q: Who rushed for two touchdowns in the fourth quarter of the 1995 Orange Bowl?

15 Q: What Husker running back owns an NU rushing record, carrying the ball 294 yards in a single game?

1 A: Johnny Rodgers

2 A: Rich Glover

3 A: Mike Rozier

4 A: Mike Rozier

5 A: Dave Rimington

6 A: Kenny Walker

7 A: Tommie Frazier

8 A: Eric Piatkowski

9 A: Derek Brown and Calvin Jones

10 A: "Marvelous" Jarvis Redwine

11 A: 20

12 A: Mike Rozier

13 A: Omaha Technical

14 A: Cory Schlesinger

15 A: Calvin Jones

16 Q: What NU quarterback tops the charts in the Husker stats for total yards and touchdowns?

17 Q: What football player's jersey was taken out of retirement so that his son could wear the same number?

18 Q: What rushing duo was nicknamed the "We Backs" at NU?

19 Q: What NU basketball player was picked in the first round of the1991 NBA draft by the Seattle Supersonics?

20 Q: Who at NU carried the nickname of "Tough Tony"?

21 Q: Which Nebraska defender sacked Miami's quarterback Frank Costa for a safety and the only points scored in the third quarter?

22 Q: Which Nebraska quarterback came to the Huskers from Green Bay, Wisconsin?

23 Q: Who was the first freshman to start at quarterback for Nebraska?

24 Q: Who was NU's first Afro-American "regular" quarterback?

25 Q: Which NU quarterback took over for an injured Tommie Frazier in the 1994 season?

26 Q: How many touchdowns did Husker great Mike Rozier score against Oklahoma during his Nebraska career: 1, 5, 8 or 10?

27 Q: Which Husker was the quarterback sack leader for his career?

28 Q: Which NU football great wore the nickname "The Jet"?

29 Q: Which Husker carried the nickname "Dodger" during his Nebraska career?

16 A: Dave Humm

17 A: Johnny Rodgers

18 A: Calvin Jones and Derek Brown

19 A: Rich King

20 A: Tony Davis

21 A: Dwayne Harris

22 A: Jerry Tagge

23 A: Tommie Frazier

24 A: Turner Gill

25 A: Brook Berringer

26 A: 1

27 A: Trev Alberts with 29 1/2 sacks

28 A: Johnny Rodgers

29 A: Roger Craig

30 Q: What position did Dave Hoppen play on the Husker basketball team?

31 Q: Which NU football great had the nickname "The Flyer"?

32 Q: Name two of the three NU quarterbacks to be named All-Americans.

33 Q: Name the three NU athletes that have been honored with the Lombardi Trophy.

34 Q: Which Husker scored the winning touchdown in the 1971 Orange Bowl victory?

35 Q: Who was the freshman running back who practically saved the Huskers from defeat against UCLA in 1993?

36 Q: Who was the first Husker to leave school early to enter into the NFL draft?

37 Q: Which Husker scored the 2 point conversion in the 1995 Orange Bowl that tied the game after Schlesinger's first touchdown?

38 Q: Name the player who made 22 tackles for Nebraska in the 1971 "Game of the Century" against Oklahoma.

39 Q: What was Calvin Jones' number?

40 Q: What position did Rich King play on the Nebraska basketball team?

41 Q: What NU football player was nicknamed "Endzone"?

42 Q: Which Husker athlete was named UPI Lineman-of-the-year in 1994?

43 Q: Name the quarterback that decided to transfer in 1994 to Nebraska after spending two years at Stanford University.

44 Q: What position did Mark Schellen play for the Huskers?

30 A: Center

31 A: Wingback Irving Fryar

32 A: Jerry Tagge, Dave Humm, Vince Ferragamo and Steve Taylor

33 A: Rich Glover, Dave Rimington and Dean Steinkuhler

34 A: Jerry Tagge scored on a one yard dive into the end zone.

35 A: Lawrence Phillips

36 A: Johnny Mitchell left in 1992 and was drafted by the Jets.

37 A: Eric Alford

38 A: Rich Glover

39 A: 44

40 A: Center

41 A: Keith "Endzone" Jones

42 A: Zach Wiegert

43 A: Scott Frost

44 A: Fullback

45 Q: Name the running back from Omaha Central High School who joined the Huskers in 1995?

46 Q: What Nebraska player won the Outland and Rockne Trophies in 1971?

47 Q: Who scored the winning touchdown in the 1971 Nebraska/Oklahoma game?

48 Q: Which NU back rushed for 205 yards and scored one touchdown in the 1983 Nebraska/Oklahoma game?

49 Q: Name the slugger who helped Nebraska win the 1950 Big Seven baseball title.

50 Q: Who won the Outland Trophy in 1992?

51 Q: Which NU Lombardi and Outland Trophy winner came to Nebraska weighing 220 pounds and left at 274 pounds?

52 Q: Who is the only player in NCAA history to win the Outland Trophy twice?

53 Q: Which NU baseball player was chosen first overall in the 1995 Major League Baseball draft?

54 Q: What position did All-American Neil Smith play on the Husker football team?

55 Q: Which Husker was the intended receiver for the 2 point conversion pass in the closing minutes of the 1984 Orange Bowl?

56 Q: Who was the freshman quarterback that keyed the victory for Miami in the 1984 Orange bowl?

57 Q: Who carried the nickname of "The Jet" during his NU days?

58 Q: What two sports did Erick Strickland play while at NU?

45 A: Ahman Green

46 A: Larry Jacobson

47 A: Jeff Kinney

48 A: Mike Rozier

49 A: Bob Cerv

50 A: Will Shields

51 A: Dean Steinkuhler

52 A: Dave Rimington

53 A: Darin Erstad

54 A: Defensive tackle

55 A: Irving Fryar

56 A: Bernie Kosar

57 A: Johnny Rodgers

58 A: Baseball and Basketball

59 Q: What did Johnny Rodgers do following his famous punt return against Oklahoma?

60 Q: Which NU quarterback's career pass completion record was broken by Dave Humm?

61 Q: Which quarterback's single season pass completion record was broken by Vince Ferragamo?

62 Q: Who had the nickname "Train Wreck" at Nebraska?

63 Q: How many touchdown receptions did Johnny Rodgers have in his Nebraska career: 20, 22, 26 or 29?

64 Q: Which Husker wingback broke Guy Ingles' career record for yardage gained by pass receptions?

65 Q: What position did Johnny Rodgers play for the Huskers?

66 Q: True or False. Eric Piatkowski signed a 5 year deal with the NBA team that originally drafted him.

67 Q: What position did Jerry Tagge play for the Huskers?

68 Q: What position did Gregg Barrios play for the Huskers?

69 Q: What running back had the nickname "Lighthorse" at NU?

70 Q: What position did Jeff Kinney play on the Husker football team?

71 Q: What position did Trev Alberts play for the Huskers?

72 Q: From what city was Husker gymnast Phil Cohoy recruited?

73 Q: Is the Husker great Dave Humm right or left handed?

74 Q: Who was the Husker that led the Big Eight in scoring during the 1972 season?

59 A: He vomited from exhaustion.

60 A: Jerry Tagge

61 A: Jerry Tagge

62 A: Tom "Train Wreck" Novak

63 A: 26

64 A: Johnny Rodgers

65 A: Wingback

66 A: False, Indiana traded Eric to the L.A. Clippers.

67 A: Quarterback

68 A: Place kicker

69 A: Harry Wilson

70 A: I-back or running back

71 A: Linebacker

72 A: Omaha, NE

73 A: Dave is a lefty

74 A: Johnny Rodgers

75 Q: What was Husker great Charlie Winters' nickname?

76 Q: Which Husker football player was the Big Eight scoring leader in 1982?

77 Q: Which Husker defensive back had the most interception returns for touchdowns in his career: Dave Mason or Larry Wachholtz?

78 Q: Who had the nickname "Zippety" for the Husker football team?

79 Q: Which NU linebacker from the 1980's always referred to Memorial Stadium as "Our House"?

80 Q: From what city was Husker gymnast Jim Hartung recruited?

81 Q: Who was named the MVP of the "Game of the Century" in 1971?

82 Q: Name one of the two All-American middle guards from Devaney's Huskers.

83 Q: Which Big Eight School did Nebraska native Gale Sayers choose over Nebraska?

84 Q: Which key Husker defender was knocked out of the game in the first quarter of the 1993 OU game?

85 Q: Jeff Kinney gained 171 yards in the Game of the Century. What was his longest touchdown run; 3, 35, or 68 yards?

86 Q: Which NU football player left school early in 1993 to enter the NFL draft?

87 Q: What Omaha high school did Husker great Dave Hoppen attend?

88 Q: What two sports did Darrin Erstad play at Nebraska?

75 A: "Choo Choo"

76 A: Mike Rozier

77 A: Dave Mason had 3

78 A: Fred "Zippety" Duda

79 A: Broderick Thomas

80 A: Omaha, NE

81 A: Jerry Tagge

82 A: Wayne Meylan and Rich Glover

83 A: Kansas

84 A: Trev Alberts

85 A: 3 yards

86 A: Calvin Jones

87 A: Omaha Benson high school

88 A: Baseball and Football

89 Q: Name the 1961 co-captain for the Husker football team who later played center for the Minnesota Vikings.

90 Q: Who was called the "Sandman" at Nebraska?

91 Q: Name the 1960 Husker co-captain who had a great career as a defensive back in the NFL.

92 Q: What is Johnny Rodgers' most famous play?

93 Q: Name the quarterback who moved to tight end in 1969.

89 A: Mick Tinglehoff

90 A: Broderick Thomas

91 A: Pat Fischer

92 A: A 77 yard punt return in the 1971 OU game

93 A: Frank Patrick

67 Q: What position did Jerry Tagge play for the
Huskers?

2. Coaches

108 Q: What item of clothing does Danny Nee
promote: shirts, socks, hats or ties?

94 Q: From what college did Tom Osborne graduate in 1959?

95 Q: What was Danny Nee's first year as the NU basketball coach?

96 Q: What football coach has led NU to the most Big Eight titles?

97 Q: What football coach has served the longest in NU history?

98 Q: Who served as Tommie Frazier's mentor and quarterback coach?

99 Q: Which Husker football coach holds the record for the most NU victories?

100 Q: Who is the Huskers Baseball Head Coach?

101 Q: Who is the only Nebraska football coach to defeat a #1 team?

102 Q: Which NU football coach holds the Big Eight record for most victories in the conference?

103 Q: Who replaced Bob Devaney as Head Coach for the Huskers?

104 Q: Whose position did Bill Byrne take in 1993?

105 Q: When was Bob Devaney named National Coach of the Year?

106 Q: At what University did Bob Devaney coach prior to coming to NU in 1962?

107 Q: How many seasons has John Sanders coached the Husker Baseball team: 3, 7, 13 or 18?

108 Q: What item of clothing does Danny Nee promote: shirts, socks, hats or ties?

94 A: Hastings College

95 A: 1986-87 season

96 A: Tom Osborne

97 A: Tom Osborne

98 A: Turner Gill

99 A: Tom Osborne

100 A: John Sanders

101 A: Tom Osborne

102 A: Tom Osborne has recorded 219 victories as of the end of the 1994 season.

103 A: Assistant Coach Tom Osborne

104 A: Athletic Director Bob Devaney

105 A: Oddly enough, he never was named Coach of the Year.

106 A: Wyoming

107 A: As of the end of the 1995 season: 18

108 A: Ties

109 Q: What Husker coach played professionally for the San Francisco 49ers?

110 Q: What position did Tom Osborne play in college?

111 Q: What Big Eight school tried to recruit Tom Osborne away from the Huskers after the 1978 season?

112 Q: What is the least number of games in a season NU football has won under the direction of Tom Osborne?

113 Q: What subject did Tom Osborne teach at the University of Nebraska?

114 Q: What team handed both Devaney and Osborne their biggest margin of defeat?

115 Q: In what year did Tom Osborne join the coaching staff at NU?

116 Q: Name the Husker's coach for both the men's and women's swim team.

117 Q: In what subject is Tom Osborne's doctorate?

118 Q: Who has made NU's weight training program the envy of all other college teams?

119 Q: What is the title of Tom Osborne's autobiography?

120 Q: What NU coach has a national record 13 bowl game losses?

121 Q: How many times in Tom Osborne's career has a Husker football team been shut out?

122 Q: Name the head coach for both the men's and women's track and field teams.

123 Q: In what year was the highest number of points scored in a season by a Bob Devaney coached football team?

109 A: Tom Osborne

110 A: Quarterback

111 A: The University of Colorado

112 A: The Huskers have won just 8 games on four separate occasions.

113 A: Educational Psychology

114 A: Oklahoma

115 A: He joined as a volunteer coach in 1962

116 A: Cal Bentz

117 A: Educational Psychology

118 A: Boyd Epley

119 A: More Than Winning

120 A: Tom Osborne

121 A: Two times

122 A: Gary Pepin

123 A: 1971, Huskers scored 507 points

124 Q: Which NU football coach was named both High School and College Athlete of the Year by the Omaha World Herald?

125 Q: Many experts refer to which Nebraska football team as the greatest team ever?

126 Q: Were any Huskers named team captain two years in a row for a Tom Osborne coached Nebraska team?

127 Q: What was significant about Nebraska's National Championship in 1995 under the direction of Tom Osborne?

128 Q: Which NU coach has taken the Huskers to the most bowl games?

129 Q: How many Husker teams went to bowl games in Devaney's first five years as head coach for NU?

130 Q: Name the only Big Eight team that has not defeated a Devaney or Osborne coached Nebraska team.

131 Q: Which Big Eight teams have never defeated a Tom Osborne coached Husker team?

132 Q: In Bob Devaney's eleven years as head coach for the Huskers, how many non-conference opponents defeated Nebraska: 1,3,7 or 11?

133 Q: What year was Bob Devaney's first conference championship with the Cornhuskers?

134 Q: What NU basketball coach had the nickname "Slippery Joe"?

135 Q: Who is the Athletic Director for the University?

136 Q: Which NU assistant football coach was a co-captain for the 1965 Husker team?

137 Q: Which school tried to hire assistant football coach Ron Brown away following the 1993 season?

124 A: Tom Osborne

125 A: The 1971 National Championship team

126 A: No

127 A: It was the Huskers' first with Osborne as their coach.

128 A: Tom Osborne has in every year he has coached.

129 A: All five

130 A: Oklahoma State

131 A: Kansas, Kansas State and Oklahoma State

132 A: Three

133 A: 1963

134 A: Joe Cipriano

135 A: Bill Byrne

136 A: Frank Solich

137 A: Florida State

138 Q: What position did John Melton coach for the Husker football team?

139 Q: How many times have Tom Osborne's Huskers been tied?

140 Q: What is the correct pronunciation of Tom Osborne's name?

141 Q: Who was named head coach for the NU men's basketball team following the death of Joe Cipriano?

142 Q: What promotion did Tom Osborne receive with the NU football program in 1972?

143 Q: To what bowl did Bob Devaney lead his first Husker team?

144 Q: Name the Big Eight school defensive coordinator for which Charlie McBride played.

145 Q: After which season were petitions circulated around Omaha calling for Bob Devaney's resignation?

146 Q: What is Tom Osborne's favorite pastime off the football field?

147 Q: Whose coaching philosophy is, "It isn't winning that matters as much as the process of athletics"?

148 Q: How many years did Moe Iba lead the Husker men's basketball team?

149 Q: Name the 1965 co-captain of the NU football team that later returned as an assistant coach.

150 Q: How many conference titles did Devaney win at Nebraska?

151 Q: What were E.O "Jumbo" Stiehm's football teams at Nebraska nicknamed?

138 A: John served as a linebackers coach.

139 A: Three times: Oklahoma State, LSU and Colorado

140 A: Oz-bern as opposed to Oz-born

141 A: Moe Iba

142 A: Assistant head coach

143 A: The Gotham Bowl

144 A: Colorado

145 A: After posting his second 6-4 season in 1968

146 A: Trout fishing

147 A: Tom Osborne

148 A: Six

149 A: Frank Solich

150 A: Eight

151 A: "The Stiehmrollers"

152 Q: Which Nebraska legend married his college sweetheart Phyllis Wiley?

153 Q: How many times have the Huskers been left out of a bowl game with Tom Osborne as head coach?

154 Q: In Moe Iba's six years at the helm of the NU basketball team, how many times did the Huskers advance to post-season play?

155 Q: Who was Nebraska's first full-time strength coach?

156 Q: What colors do the football coaches wear during away games?

157 Q: Who was the Husker football coach when the Memorial Stadium sellout streak began?

158 Q: When was Bob Devaney's first undefeated season at NU?

159 Q: To how many undefeated seasons did Bob Devaney lead the Husker football team?

160 Q: When was Bob Devaney's first undefeated Big Eight season?

161 Q: When was Tom Osborne's first undefeated Big Eight season?

162 Q: Who is the Huskers 24th men's basketball coach in Nebraska school history?

163 Q: How many losing seasons did Bob Devaney have in his 30 years of coaching?

164 Q: How many times did Devaney's Husker quarterbacks throw for over 300 yards in a single game: 4, 7, 11 or 14?

165 Q: Was it the Devaney or the Osborne era team that gave up the fewest touchdowns in a single season?

152 A: Bob Devaney

153 A: Zero

154 A: Four

155 A: Boyd Epley

156 A: Scarlet shirts and Cream colored pants

157 A: Bob Devaney

158 A: 1970

159 A: Two: 1970 and 1971

160 A: 1963

161 A: 1981

162 A: Danny Nee

163 A: None

164 A: Only 4

165 A: Osborne's 1981 Huskers gave up only 9 TD's.

166 Q: Who was called the "Fat Fox" at Nebraska?

167 Q: What two coaches have won national championships for Nebraska's football program?

168 Q: How many 20 win seasons has Danny Nee collected at NU?

169 Q: What Husker football coach is quoted saying, "Nebraska has no true football rivals"?

170 Q: True of False. All three of NU's baseball coaches are Nebraska natives.

171 Q: Who is the only Big Eight football opponent to hold a winning edge in their series with Osborne's Huskers?

172 Q: With what Big Eight opponent did Bob Devaney have the least success?

173 Q: Who is the Head Coach of the NU mens Basketball team?

174 Q: Which NU coach appears on the cover of the January 9, 1995 issue of Sports Illustrated?

175 Q: True or False. Tom Osborne has never been photographed smiling.

176 Q: Who is responsible for dubbing the trio of Rozier, Fryar and Gill as the "triplets"?

177 Q: Bill "Thunder" Thornton was the star of which coach's first road victory?

178 Q: Name the winningest wrestling coach in NU history.

179 Q: Sports Illustrated said, "If you're Tom Osborne looking to win your first national title, who you gonna call?"

180 Q: Who is NU's Athletic Director Emeritus?

166 A: Associate A.D. Don Bryant

167 A: Bob Devaney and Tom Osborne

168 A: Four

169 A: Tom Osborne

170 A: True

171 A: Oklahoma

172 A: Oklahoma

173 A: Danny Nee

174 A: Tom Osborne

175 A: False, Tom Osborne was caught smiling in his 4th grade class photo.

176 A: OU coach Barry Switzer

177 A: Bob Devaney

178 A: Tim Neumann

179 A: Tommie Frazier

180 A: Bob Devaney.

181 Q: True or False. The best time to reach Husker baseball coach John Sanders is at the office between 9-11 a.m.

182 Q: True or False. Did Bob Devaney coach under Duffy Daugherty?

183 Q: What is the first name of Tom Osborne's wife?

184 Q: At which university did Danny Nee coach prior to coming to Nebraska?

181 A: True

182 A: True.

183 A: Nancy

184 A: Ohio University

99 Q: Which Husker football coach holds the record for the most NU victories?

3. General

231 Q: What nickname did NU fans give to Husker great Eric Piatkowski?

185 Q: Name the four schools that joined the Big Eight in 1994 to form the Big Twelve Conference.

186 Q: What football team spoiled NU's chance at an undefeated season and a national championship in 1993?

187 Q: What is NU football's top defensive unit at Nebraska nicknamed?

188 Q: What nickname did the 1983 Husker football team earn for their high scoring capabilities?

189 Q: True or False. One of the previous nicknames for Nebraska was the "Antelopes."

190 Q: How many points did the Huskers score in the fourth quarter of the 1995 Orange Bowl?

191 Q: True or False. Every time the Huskers completed a 13-0 Season, they were awarded a National Championship?

192 Q: What is the name of the home field for the Husker Baseball team?

193 Q: Name two of the several nicknames used prior to the adoption of the name "Cornhuskers."

194 Q: Whose number was first retired by the NU football team?

195 Q: True or False. Nebraska and Oklahoma will still play each other in football on an annual basis in the Big Twelve.

196 Q: Outside linebacker Trev Alberts was chosen in the 1994 draft by which NFL franchise?

197 Q: What are the official school colors of the Nebraska Cornhuskers?

198 Q: In what NCAA athletic conference do the Nebraska Cornhuskers compete?

185 A. Baylor, Texas A&M, Texas Tech and Texas

186 A: Florida State University

187 A: Blackshirts

188 A: The Scoring Explosion!

189 A: True

190 A: 15

191 A: True

192 A: Buck Beltzer Stadium

193 A: Black Knights, Bugeaters, Rattlesnake Boys, Old Gold Knights and Antelopes

194 A: Tom Novak's number 60

195 A: False

196 A: Indianapolis Colts

197 A: Scarlet and Cream

198 A: The Big Eight

199 Q: In what city do the Huskers play their home games?

200 Q: What is the nickname of the University of Nebraska/Lincoln athletic teams?

201 Q: How many games did the NU volleyball team lose in the 1994 regular season?

202 Q: What was Nebraska's first bowl win?

203 Q: After falling behind 17-0 in the first quarter of the 1984 Orange Bowl, when did the Huskers gain a lead in the battle against Miami?

204 Q: In what stadium was the 1962 Gotham Bowl played?

205 Q: Which bowl game win gave Nebraska its first national championship?

206 Q: What famous figure flew to Lincoln to pay tribute to the 1970 National Champion NU football team?

207 Q: What color is the artificial turf in Memorial Stadium?

208 Q: What will the Big Eight conference be named after the additions of the Texas schools in 1996?

209 Q: Where does the Husker volleyball team play its home games?

210 Q: In what city is Big Eight opponent Colorado located?

211 Q: How many divisions will there be for Football and Men's and Women's Basketball in the Big Twelve conference?

212 Q: How many Heisman Trophy winners have played at the University?

213 Q: Which team gained the most offensive yards in the 1995 Orange Bowl?

199 A: Lincoln

200 A: Cornhuskers/Huskers

201 A: None

202 A: NU defeated Miami in the 1962 Gotham Bowl.

203 A: They never did

204 A: Yankee Stadium in New York City

205 A: The Orange Bowl victory over LSU in 1971

206 A: President Richard Nixon

207 A: Green

208 A: The Big Twelve

209 A: Nebraska Coliseum

210 A: Boulder, CO

211 A: Two

212 A: Two; Johnny Rodgers and Mike Rozier

213 A: Nebraska

214 Q: Where did the Huskers hold their victory rally after returning to Lincoln from the 1995 Orange Bowl?

215 Q: Name the two Nebraska mascots.

216 Q: What percent of the NU football players in 1982 attended Nebraska high schools: 20, 30,50 or 60 percent?

217 Q: Name the voice of the men's basketball team on the Nebraska Sports Network.

218 Q: Who replaced Lyle Bremser on KFAB radio to broadcast the NU football games?

219 Q: What was Lyle Bremser's famous quote after a great play by the Husker football team?

220 Q: What are the instant replay boards located in Memorial Stadium called?

221 Q: Where is the Big Eight basketball tournament held annually?

222 Q: Where is the Big Eight conference office?

223 Q: Name the radio personality with the famous expression: touchdown, touchdown, touchdown!

224 Q: What is the name of the Indoor facility for the NU track team?

225 Q: What is written on the south end zone in Memorial Stadium?

226 Q: What is written on the north end zone in Memorial Stadium?

227 Q: Nebraska originated from the Otoe Indian word "Nebraska." What does that word mean?

228 Q: What Omaha high school produced the most recruits for the Husker football team in 1995?

214 A: Devaney Sports Center

215 A: Harry and Herbie

216 A: 60 percent

217 A: Kent Pavelka

218 A: Kent Pavelka

219 A: Man, woman and child

220 A: Husker Vision

221 A: Kemper Arena in Kansas City, Missouri

222 A: Kansas City, Missouri

223 A: Kent Pavelka

224 A: Bob Devaney Sports Center

225 A: Nebraska

226 A: Huskers

227 A: Flat water

228 A: Burke High School

229 Q: What was the final score of the 1995 Orange Bowl?

230 Q: What state produced the most recruits in 1995 for the Husker football team?

231 Q: What nickname did NU fans give to Husker great Eric Piatkowski?

232 Q: What number did Mike Rozier wear for the Huskers?

233 Q: What number did Turner Gill wear for Nebraska?

234 Q: What position did Johnny Rodgers play for the Huskers?

235 Q: Within one inch, how tall is Johnny Rodgers?

236 Q: What position did Jeff Kinney play in high school?

237 Q: Who were the brothers from Washington D.C. that were an incredible defensive duo for the Huskers football team in the early 1980's?

238 Q: Name the high school All-American in football and basketball that played tight end for the Huskers in the 1980's.

239 Q: Why did Turner Gill give up a professional career in football?

240 Q: Name two of the three Damkroger family members who played football at Nebraska.

241 Q: What NU quarterback quit professional football for a shot in the major leagues of baseball?

242 Q: What symbol is displayed on the side of the Husker football helmet?

243 Q: What color is the face mask on a Husker football helmet?

229 A: Nebraska 24, Miami 17

230 A: Nebraska with seven

231 A: The Polish Rifle

232 A: 30

233 A: 12

234 A: Wingback

235 A: 5'9"

236 A: Quarterback

237 A: Jimmy and Toby Williams

238 A: Jamie Williams

239 A: Recurring concussions

240 A: Steve, Maury and Ralph

241 A: Turner Gill

242 A: An "N"

243 A: Red

244 Q: Where is the third largest populated area in Nebraska on game day Saturdays in the fall?

245 Q: What is the name of the retail shop directly west of Memorial Stadium?

246 Q: Who are the "Big Three" sports announcers on Nebraska's Football Network?

247 Q: What is the policy on the use of umbrellas in Memorial Stadium?

248 Q: Where are the girls the fairest and the boys the squarest?

249 Q: What food chain sells Husker burritos in Memorial Stadium?

250 Q: Who presented the 1971 national championship plaque to the Huskers?

251 Q: In what city is Big Eight opponent Missouri located?

252 Q: In what city is Big Eight opponent Kansas located?

253 Q: In what city is Big Eight opponent Oklahoma State located?

254 Q: In what city is Big Eight opponent Oklahoma located?

255 Q: In what city is Big Eight opponent Iowa State located?

256 Q: In what city is Big Eight opponent Kansas State located?

257 Q: How many states are represented in the Big Eight conference?

258 Q: How many states are represented in the Big Twelve conference?

259 Q: What two schools won every Big Eight football title from 1962 through 1988?

244 A: Memorial Stadium

245 A: Big Red Shop

246 A: Gary Sadlemyer, Kent Pavelka and Jim Rose

247 A: They are prohibited

248 A: Nebraska University

249 A: Amigos

250 A: President Richard Nixon

251 A: Columbia, MO

252 A: Lawrence, KS

253 A: Oklahoma City, OK

254 A: Norman, OK

255 A: Ames, IA

256 A: Manhattan, KS

257 A: Six

258 A: Seven

259 A: Nebraska and Oklahoma

260 Q: What has been traditionally Nebraska's last football game of the Big Eight conference?

261 Q: Why is the top defensive unit at Nebraska called the Blackshirts?

262 Q: What was known as the "big sport" on the University of Nebraska campus in the late 1940's?

263 Q: Which Huskers were known as "Earth, Wind and Fryar"?

264 Q: How many draft picks in the NFL has Nebraska averaged since the 1960's: under or over five?

265 Q: Why was the NU football team declared the Big Eight champions of 1972?

266 Q: How was the Bob Devaney Sports Center financed?

267 Q: If someone from Hastings needed to call the Nebraska athletics department, what area code would be used?

268 Q: True of False. One of the earlier nicknames for Nebraska was the "Rattle Snake Boys."

269 Q: True of False. One of the earlier nicknames for Nebraska was the "Red Knights."

270 Q: True of False. One of the earlier nicknames for Nebraska was the Sooners.

271 Q: Name two of the non-conference opponents in 1995 for the Husker football team.

272 Q: True of False. Nebraska and Oklahoma will participate in the same division of the Big Twelve conference.

273 Q: True or False. Nebraska's "official" school colors are Crimson and Cream.

260 A: Oklahoma

261 A: They wear black jerseys in practice.

262 A: Men's basketball

263 A: Turner Gill, Mike Rozier and Irving Fryar

264 A: Over five

265 A: Oklahoma was placed on probation.

266 A: A special cigarette tax

267 A: 402

268 A: True

269 A: False, It was the "Black Knights."

270 A: False, (If you answered true you should be flogged)

271 A: Michigan State, Arizona State, Pacific and Washington State

272 A: False

273 A: False, they are scarlet and cream.

274 Q: In what year was Husker Vision installed in Memorial Stadium?

275 Q: True or False. Within three to five years sky boxes will be added to Memorial Stadium.

276 Q: True or False. Tom Osborne would win the popular vote in the state of Nebraska if he ran for the President of the United States.

274 A: 1994

275 A: True

276 A: True. To say otherwise would be un-American.

212 Q: **How many Heisman Trophy winners have played at the University?**

4. History

286 Q: Which Nebraska football player is the only one in school history to be named an All-American in his sophomore year?

277 Q: How many times have the Huskers competed in the Rose Bowl?

278 Q: Who was the football opponent for the Huskers 200th consecutive home sellout game?

279 Q: What football teams finished first through third in the final AP poll of 1971?

280 Q: True or False. The Hurricanes' only loss on their home turf in the last decade was to the Nebraska Cornhuskers.

281 Q: Which Husker is the only player in school history to win the Outland Trophy in two consecutive years?

282 Q: Which Huskers were named Big Eight Offensive Football Players of the Year in 1992?

283 Q: Where was the 1977 Liberty Bowl played?

284 Q: Which Husker was named football's Big Eight Freshman-of-the-Year in 1992.

285 Q: Name two of the three Huskers selected in the first round of the NFL draft in 1972?

286 Q: Which Nebraska football player is the only one in school history to be named an All-American in his sophomore year?

287 Q: In the year that Mike Rozier won the Heisman Trophy, which Husker teammate finished fourth in the balloting?

288 Q: How many touchdowns did Johnny Rodgers record in his last game as a Husker?

289 Q: Which team did NU play in a bowl game three times in the 1980's?

290 Q: In the 1973 Orange Bowl against Notre Dame, for how many of NU's 40 points was Johnny Rodgers responsible?

277 A: Once, in 1941

278 A: Colorado

279 A: Nebraska, Oklahoma and Colorado

280 A: False, Miami also lost to Washington in their 1994 home opener

281 A: Dave Rimington won this award in 1981 and 1982

282 A: Calvin Jones and Derek Brown

283 A: Memphis, TN

284 A: Tommie Frazier

285 A: Jerry Tagge, Larry Jacobson and Jeff Kinney

286 A: Bobby Reynolds

287 A: Turner Gill

288 A: Rodgers scored 4 TD's in the 1973 Orange Bowl

289 A: Louisiana State University

290 A: 24 points on 4 touchdowns

291 Q: When was the last year a Husker men's gymnastics team at the University of Nebraska has won a national championship?

292 Q: How many bowl games did the Huskers play in 1974?

293 Q: How many victories did Gale Sayers lead the Kansas Jayhawks to against the Huskers?

294 Q: How many times did Colorado defeat Nebraska in the 70's?

295 Q: When was Kansas States last football victory over the Huskers?

296 Q: Who played in the first ever Kickoff Classic?

297 Q: Who was NU's first opponent after Devaney took over as the Huskers head coach?

298 Q: Who won the Big Six title in its first year of existence?

299 Q: When was Nebraska's last undefeated and untied season prior to the 1994 championship season?

300 Q: Where was the 1976 Bluebonnet Bowl game held?

301 Q: When was the first time that a Nebraska football team played outside the United States?

302 Q: Which team tied the Cornhuskers 21-21 in the 1970 season to keep the Nebraska team from recording a perfect season?

303 Q: Prior to the 1995 Orange Bowl victory, when was the last bowl game victory for the Huskers?

304 Q: In what year did Memorial Stadium open?

305 Q: How many times did the Huskers sack the Miami quarterback, Frank Costa, in the 1995 Orange Bowl?

291 A: 1994

292 A: Two. The Cotton Bowl following the 1973 season and the Sugar Bowl on New Year's Eve following the 1974 season

293 A: None

294 A: Zero times

295 A: A 12-0 shutout in 1968

296 A: Nebraska defeated Penn State in 1983.

297 A: Division 1-AA South Dakota

298 A: Nebraska

299 A: 1971

300 A: Houston, TX

301 A: In 1992 NU played Kansas State in Tokyo, Japan.

302 A: Southern California

303 A: 1987's Sugar Bowl win over LSU

304 A: 1923

305 A: 5 times

306 Q: What plan put running backs Roger Craig and Mike Rozier in the same backfield in 1982?

307 Q: In the 1971 Nebraska/Oklahoma match-up, which team led 17-14 at the half?

308 Q: When did Tom Osborne's Huskers first beat Oklahoma?

309 Q: What controversial play allowed Penn State to score on the winning drive in the 1982 match-up against the Huskers?

310 Q: Who was the Canadian Football League's first deaf football player?

311 Q: Which Husker was the first in school history to win the Nissen Award?

312 Q: Who did Nebraska defeat in the finals of the 1994 Big Eight Basketball Tournament?

313 Q: Name Nebraska's second Heisman Trophy winner.

314 Q: What player from Oklahoma did Johnny Rodgers beat out for the Heisman Trophy?

315 Q: Name the huge guard taken in the first round of the 1964 NFL draft by the Philadelphia Eagles.

316 Q: Who is the only Husker quarterback to lead an NFL team to the Super Bowl?

317 Q: Name the 1977-79 split end and punter who later played several seasons with the Houston Oilers.

318 Q: Where was the 1965 Cotton Bowl played?

319 Q: Name the NU defensive tackle who scored a safety for the Chicago Bears in their Super Bowl victory over New England.

320 Q: Who scored the first touchdown in the Nebraska/Oklahoma game in 1971?

306 A: Moving Craig to fullback allowed both to share the backfield.

307 A: Oklahoma

308 A: In 1978

309 A: The officials ruled a pass complete that was later confirmed by video tape to be caught out of bounds.

310 A: Nebraska's Kenny Walker

311 A: Jim Hartung

312 A: Oklahoma State

313 A: Mike Rozier

314 A: Greg Pruitt

315 A: Bob Brown

316 A: Vince Ferragamo

317 A: Tim Smith

318 A: Dallas, Texas

319 A: Henry Waechter

320 A: Johnny Rodgers on a 72 yard punt return

321 Q: Which Husker had four touchdowns in the NU/OU game in 1971?

322 Q: Who had the most total offensive yardage in the 1971 Nebraska/Oklahoma game?

323 Q: How many times did the Blackshirts cause Oklahoma to fumble in Osborne's first victory over the Sooners: two, four, six or nine?

324 Q: In the 1967-68 basketball season, NU had two 1,000 point scorers in the team's lineup for the first time ever. Who were these men?

325 Q: Name the quarterback who replaced Fred Duda during the 1964 season after Duda broke his leg in a game against Iowa State.

326 Q: Who won the game in the first football meeting between Nebraska and Notre Dame?

327 Q: Who won the game in the first football meeting between Nebraska and Colorado?

328 Q: Who was the All-American linebacker recruited in 1968 from Burke High School in Omaha, Nebraska?

329 Q: Who is the football co-captain from 1978 with the nickname "smiling assassin"?

330 Q: Name the only NU football player in school history with a last name starting with the letter "Q."

331 Q: Nebraska has produced more Outland Trophy winners than any other school. How many are credited to Huskers?

332 Q: Which "Big Twelve" expansion team did the Huskers play in the 1988 Kickoff classic?

333 Q: Which player's 92 yard kickoff return helped spark the victory over Miami in the 1962 Gotham Bowl?

321 A: Jeff Kinney

322 A: Oklahoma with a 467-362 edge

323 A: Nine

324 A: Tom Baack and Stuart Lantz

325 A: Bob Churchich

326 A: Nebraska 20-19 in 1915

327 A: NU won 10-0

328 A: Jerry Murtaugh

329 A: George Andrews

330 A: Jeff Quinn

331 A: Seven trophies by six players

332 A: Texas A&M

333 A: Willie Ross

334 Q: Where was the 1969 Sun Bowl played?

335 Q: Name the Nebraska sophomore running back who rushed for 102 yards in the 1985 Sugar Bowl?

336 Q: Which Alabama quarterback keyed the victory for the Tide in the 1966 Orange Bowl?

337 Q: What offensive formation did Stanford employ in the 1941 Rose Bowl game?

338 Q: Which Husker's one yard TD carry in the fourth quarter sealed the national championship for the Huskers in the 1971 Orange Bowl?

339 Q: What was Nebraska ranked prior to the 1971 Orange Bowl?

340 Q: Who did NU play in the 1985 Sugar Bowl?

341 Q: In what year did the Memorial Stadium sellout streak begin?

342 Q: How many teams tied Nebraska during the regular season of the 1971 National Championship season?

343 Q: What team defeated NU in the 1954 Orange Bowl?

344 Q: Where was the 1967 Sugar Bowl played?

345 Q: Which team did NU defeat (40-6) in the 1973 Orange Bowl?

346 Q: When was Tom Osborne's first undefeated season?

347 Q: In what city was the 1975 Fiesta Bowl played in?

348 Q: Who did Nebraska lose to in the 1979 Orange Bowl?

349 Q: When was the last time two Big Eight teams played one another in the Orange Bowl?

334 A: El Paso, Texas

335 A: Doug DuBose

336 A: Steve Sloan

337 A: The T-formation

338 A: Jerry Tagge

339 A: Third

340 A: Louisiana State

341 A: 1962

342 A: None

343 A: Duke

344 A: New Orleans, LA

345 A: Notre Dame

346 A: 1994

347 A: Tempe, AZ

348 A: Oklahoma

349 A: 1979

350 Q: When was the last time the Huskers played a bowl game indoors?

351 Q: What was similar about the teams Nebraska played in the 1985 and 1987 Sugar Bowls?

352 Q: Frank Patrick was shifted from quarterback to what position during the 1969 season?

353 Q: Who took over the quarterbacking duties in 1981 for the injured Turner Gill?

354 Q: Mike Rozier tied an NCAA record with 29 touchdowns in which Husker season?

355 Q: When was the only time in the last three decades for an NU back to rush for over 200 yards against Oklahoma?

356 Q: What conference did the Huskers win to send them to the Rose Bowl in 1941?

357 Q: Who was the conference scoring leader from the 1950 Husker football team?

358 Q: What was the name of Husker great Steve Damkroger's brother who played on the 1971 championship team?

359 Q: What post-season tournament did the NU Men's basketball team participate in following the 1994-95 season?

360 Q: What Huskers were known as "Earth, Wind and Fryar"?

361 Q: Who was named the 1993 college defensive player of the year by Football News?

362 Q: In what two years did Nebraska capture the Heisman, Outland and Lombardi Trophies?

363 Q: What did the fans tear down following the 1978 football victory over Oklahoma?

350 A: The 1987 Sugar Bowl

351 A: NU played Louisiana State both years.

352 A: Tight End

353 A: Mark Mauer

354 A: 1983

355 A: 1983 when Rozier had 205 yards

356 A: The Big Six

357 A: Bobby Reynolds

358 A: Maury

359 A: National Invitation Tournament

360 A: Turner Gill, Mike Rozier and Irving Fryar

361 A: Trev Alberts

362 A: 1972 and 1983

363 A: The goal posts

364 Q: Who did Nebraska host for the 1995 homecoming football game?

365 Q: Where did Nebraska play Oklahoma in the 1995 football season?

366 Q: Who was the first Big Eight opponent for the Husker football team in 1995?

367 Q: In what year was an $800.000 sound system installed in Memorial Stadium?

368 Q: How many NU football opponents from 1994 were bowl participants?

364 A: Kansas State

365 A: Lincoln, NE (Memorial Stadium)

366 A: Oklahoma State

367 A: 1994

368 A: Seven

354 Q: Mike Rozier tied an NCAA record with 29 touchdowns in which Husker season?

5. Records

385 Q: What NU basketball player has recorded the most 30-point performances?

369 Q: What football team spoiled N.U.'s chance at an undefeated season and a national championship in 1993?

370 Q: How many national championships does the NU football team have?

371 Q: What is the NU baseball team record for most runs in a single game: 11, 18 or 28?

372 Q: Who was the running back with the most rushing attempts in a single season?

373 Q: Which NU receiver had the most touchdown receptions in his career?

374 Q: How many ball carriers rushed for over 100 yards in the 1995 Orange Bowl?

375 Q: Which NU quarterback attempted the most passes in a single game?

376 Q: Which Husker quarterback owns the record for the most completions in a single game?

377 Q: How many Big Eight tournament championships has the NU men's basketball team recorded?

378 Q: Which Husker holds the school record for most pass completions in a career at Nebraska?

379 Q: One of the greatest running backs in NU history first started as a "freshman team" quarterback . Who was this Husker?

380 Q: Which Nebraska quarterback threw for the most touchdowns in a single season?

381 Q: Which Husker player rushed for the most touchdowns in his career?

382 Q: How many points did Mike Rozier score in the 1983 season: 121, 157, 174 or 192?

369 A: Florida State University

370 A: Three

371 A: 28 against Augustana in 1980 and again in 1988 -vs.- UNO

372 A: Mike Rozier with 275 carries in 1983.

373 A: Johnny Rodgers

374 A: None

375 A: Dave Humm with 42 against Iowa State in 1972

376 A: Dave Humm had 25 completions in 1973 against Wisconsin.

377 A: One in 1994

378 A: Dave Humm completed 353 passes between 1972-74.

379 A: Jeff Kinney

380 A: Vince Ferragamo threw for 20 TD's in 1976.

381 A: Mike Rozier had 49 rushing touchdowns in his NU career.

382 A: 174 points broke the Big Eight scoring record.

383 Q: Which NU back scored the most rushing touchdowns in a season?

384 Q: Who is NU's all-time single game rushing leader?

385 Q: What NU basketball player has recorded the most 30-point performances?

386 Q: Which Nebraska back had the most rushing attempts in his career?

387 Q: Which NU running back had the best average gain per carry in a career?

388 Q: Who was the first running back to rush for over 1000 yards in a single season?

389 Q: Who had the most all-purpose running yards in NU history?

390 Q: In 1992 Calvin Jones alone rushed for more yards than how many other Big Eight teams: none, 2, 3 or 4?

391 Q: Which former Husker was the first NFL player to gain more than 1000 yards each in rushing and pass receptions in a single season?

392 Q: Which Husker had the most pass receptions in his career?

393 Q: What Nebraska pitcher won 13 games in 1993 to set a new Husker record?

394 Q: Which NU receiver had the most touchdown receptions in a single season?

395 Q: Which Nebraska running back gained the most rushing yards in a single season?

396 Q: Which Husker receiver has the record for the longest touchdown reception?

383 A: Mike Rozier had 29 in 1983.

384 A: Calvin Jones ran for 294 yards in 1991 against Kansas State.

385 A: Dave Hoppen with seven

386 A: Mike Rozier ran the ball 668 times for the Huskers.

387 A: Mike Rozier owns this record with 7.156 yards per carry.

388 A: Bobby Reynolds in 1950

389 A: Johnny Rodgers had 5586 during his career.

390 A: 4 including: Oklahoma State, Kansas State, Missouri and Colorado

391 A: Roger Craig had 2066 yards in 1985 for the San Francisco 49ers.

392 A: Johnny Rodgers had 143 pass receptions.

393 A: Troy Browhawn

394 A: Johnny Rodgers had 11 touchdown receptions in 1972.

395 A: Mike Rozier rushed for 2148 yards in 1983.

396 A: Freeman White caught a 95 yard touchdown pass in 1965 against Colorado.

397 Q: Which Husker punter had the most punts in his career?

398 Q: Who had the most punt returns for touchdowns in his career at Nebraska?

399 Q: Which Husker had the most punt returns for touchdowns in a single season?

400 Q: What Husker had the highest punt return average at 15.5 yards?

401 Q: Which Husker football player scored the most points in his career?

402 Q: Which NU baseball player owns a career record for most runs scored?

403 Q: In 1982 NU football set an NCAA record for most first downs in a game. How many first downs did they record: 25, 34, 38 or 44?

404: Q: Which NU football player scored the most points in a single game?

405 Q: Which NU football player scored the most points in a single season?

406 Q: Which Husker player gained the most offensive yards in a season?

407 Q: Nebraska football set a school record in 1992 for consecutive quarters without a turnover. How many quarters did the streak last: 12, 18 or 24?

408 Q: Which Husker football player scored the most touchdowns in a single season?

409 Q: Which Husker scored the most touchdowns in his career?

410 Q: What is the fewest yards rushing for a Nebraska football team in a single game: 15, 65, 121 or 140?

397 A: Mike Stigge had 167 punts to set the career mark.

398 A: Johnny Rodgers had seven scores on punt returns.

399 A: Johnny Rodgers had three in 1971.

400 A: Johnny Rodgers

401 A: Mike Rozier with 312 points

402 A: Ken Ramos with 204

403 A: 44 first downs against New Mexico State

404 A: Calvin Jones scored 36 points against Kansas in 1991.

405 A: Mike Rozier scored 174 points in 1982.

406 A: Jerry Tagge gained 2333 yards in 1971.

407 A: 24 quarters

408 A: Mike Rozier recorded 29 in 1983.

409 A: Mike Rozier scored 52 touchdowns.

410 A: 15 yards in 1949 against Penn State

411 Q: When was the last time that the Nebraska men's basketball team won a post-season game in the NCAA tournament?

412 Q: In what year did Nebraska football establish a new NCAA record by scoring 624 points in 12 games?

413 Q: Which Husker had 15 quarterback sacks in 1993 to establish an NU record?

414 Q: The Huskers allowed the lowest amount of total rushing yards against Kansas State in 1976. How many rushing yards did KSU gain: -49, 0, 12 or 36?

415 Q: What was the highest number of interceptions made by the NU football team in a single season: 14, 24, 30 or 36?

416 Q: Which national award did Trev Alberts win in 1993?

417 Q: In what year did the men's basketball team post the most victories?

418 Q: Who was the first Husker to win the Lombardi Trophy?

419 Q: Who was the only Nebraska football player to be named all- conference four consecutive years?

420 Q: Which Husker holds the school record for most points scored in a bowl game?

421 Q: What were the most points scored by a Big Eight opponent in Memorial Stadium?

422 Q: In what decade are the majority of the Huskers' season best records on the books for the men's basketball team?

423 Q: What is the record for most home games won in a season by the NU football team?

424 Q: At which game did NU football play before the largest crowd in school history?

411 A: They never have.

412 A: 1983

413 A: Trev Alberts

414 A: -49

415 A: 30 in 1970

416 A: The Butkus Award which is given to the top linebacker.

417 A: 1991 with 26 wins

418 A: Rich Glover

419 A: Tom Novak was honored at four different positions.

420 A: Johnny Rodgers scored 24 points in the 1973 Orange Bowl.

421 A: Oklahoma scored 48 points in 1949.

422 A: 1990's

423 A: The team has won 7 home games several times.

424 A: The 1941 Rose Bowl had a crowd of 92,000 people.

425 Q: What is the fewest number of home games won by Nebraska in a single season?

426 Q: What is the largest city in which a Big Eight school is located?

427 Q: What NU men's gymnast holds the school record for Pommel Horse, Still Rings and All-Around?

428 Q: Who upset the 1994 Husker volleyball team during their quest for a first ever national championship?

429 Q: Which NU football player holds the record for most points scored in a single game?

430 Q: How many times has Nebraska met Louisiana State in a bowl game and what is the series record?

431 Q: What was NU's record in Bob Devaney's first season with the Huskers?

432 Q: Which team defeated the NU football team in 1972 ending a 32 game unbeaten streak?

433 Q: How many overtimes were there in NU basketball's longest game in school history?

434 Q: Where would the largest weight room in the nation on a college campus be found?

435 Q: Which men's basketball player blocked the most shots in school history?

436 Q: Which team tied the Huskers in Devaney's last season?

437 Q: Who recorded 269 total offensive yards in the 34-17 Nebraska victory over Florida State in 1986?

438 Q: Which Nebraska lineman has been decorated with more awards than any other in school history?

425 A: The Huskers were winless at home in 1947, 1951 and 1957.

426 A: Lincoln, Nebraska

427 A: Jim Hartung

428 A: Penn State (1-3) in the quarter-finals of the NCAA tournament

429 A: Calvin Jones scored 36 points against Kansas in 1991.

430 A: NU defeated LSU in all 3 games: 1971, 1983 and 1987.

431 A: Nine wins and 2 losses

432 A: UCLA

433 A: Four (Alabama-Birmingham 92-84, 1979)

434 A: Memorial Stadium at NU

435 A: Rich King

436 A: Iowa State

437 A: Steve Taylor

438 A: Dave Rimington

439 Q: Into which university building is the motto, "Courage, Generosity, Fairness, Honor: These are the true rewards of manly sport" engraved?

440 Q: What is the smallest crowd to witness a Nebraska bowl game: 632, 6,160, 12,320 or 15,200?

441 Q: When was the first time the NU men's basketball team achieved back-to-back 20 win seasons?

442 Q: What distinction did the West Stadium weight room hold when it was built in 1981?

443 Q: Which Nebraska quarterback rushed for the most touchdowns in his career?

444 Q: Has Nebraska ever had two running backs rush for over 1000 yards each in the same season?

445 Q: Which Nebraska fullback had the most rushing attempts in his career: Tom Rathman, Dick Davis or Mark Schellen?

446 Q: Which NU fullback rushed for the most yards in a single season?

447 Q: Which Husker gymnast holds the men's all-around record at NU?

448 Q: Which NU receiver holds the freshman record for yards gained in pass receptions?

449 Q: Which NU receiver set a school record with 11 touchdown catches in a single season?

450 Q: Which NU receiver had the highest average gain per pass reception in a single season?

451 Q: Which of the following Huskers had the highest kickoff return average in his career: Johnny Rodgers or Pat Fischer?

439 A: Memorial Stadium

440 A: 6,160

441 A: The 1992-93 and 1993-94 seasons

442 A: It was the world's largest for athletics.

443 A: Steve Taylor rushed for 32.

444 A: Yes, Calvin Jones and Derek Brown did it in 1992.

445 A: Dick Davis

446 A: Tom Rathman

447 A: Jim Hartung

448 A: Irving Fryar

449 A: Johnny Rodgers

450 A: Johnny Mitchell in 1990

451 A: Pat Fischer

452 Q: Which Husker returned more kickoffs than any other in school history: Johnny Rodgers, Pat Fischer or Tyrone Hughes?

453 Q: The Husker football team is working on 27 straight nine-win seasons as of 1995. What is the NCAA record?

454 Q: During the 1994 Husker volleyball season, which was better: their home or away record?

455 Q: Which Husker set the school record for most yards of total offense in a game: Mike Rozier, Johnny Rodgers or Jerry Tagge?

456 Q: Who is Nebraska's all-time leading scorer: Mike Rozier, Gregg Barrios, Johnny Rodgers or John Wayne?

457 Q: What is NU football's record for consecutive games scored in: 112, 168 or 220?

458 Q: Which Nebraska defender had the most blocked punts for touchdowns in a season:; John Dutton or Wayne Meylan?

459 Q: Who holds the NU school record for the most touchdown passes in a bowl game?

460 Q: What physical characteristic did Jack Moore possess that allowed him to be eligible for the Naismith Award?

461 Q: How many field goals did Husker kicker Paul Rogers make in the first quarter of the 1969 Sun Bowl?

462 Q: How many consecutive wins did NU have over Iowa State prior to the 1992 setback: 3, 9, 14 or 28?

463 Q: Prior to NU upsetting OU in the 1959 football season, how many consecutive victories did the Sooners have: 25, 35 or 75?

464 Q: On which television network has Nebraska football had the most success?

452 A: Tyrone Hughes

453 A: That is the NCAA record.

454 A: The Huskers were a perfect 9-0 on the road but 16-1 at home.

455 A: Jerry Tagge with 319

456 A: Mike Rozier

457 A: 220

458 A: Wayne Meylan had 2 in 1966.

459 A: Bob Churchich and Craig Sundberg

460 A: He was under 6-foot tall.

461 A: An amazing four

462 A: 14

463 A: An unbelievable 75 straight wins

464 A: ESPN

465 Q: Who was the first Husker to have his jersey retired on the men's basketball team?

466 Q: What were the most victories in a single season including bowl games for the Husker football program ?

467 Q: How many perfect home seasons have the Huskers had in Memorial Stadium: 10, 12, 15 or 20?

468 Q: What was NU's most successful decade in football?

469 Q: Who won the first basketball game between Nebraska and Kansas?

470 Q: How many records did Husker hoopster Dave Hoppen break during his NU career: 8, 10, 15 or 19?

471 Q: What year will be the first football season in the Big Twelve?

472 Q: What Big Eight school has more GTE Academic All-Americans than any other?

465 A: Dave Hoppen

466 A: 13 wins in 1971 and 1994

467 A: 20 through 1994

468 A: The 1980's

469 A: Nebraska beat Kansas 48-8 in 1900.

470 A: 19

471 A: 1996

472 A: Nebraska

445 Q: Which Nebraska fullback had the most rushing attempts in his career: Tom Rathman, Dick Davis or Mark Schellen?

1. Athletes

629 Q: What position did All-American Karen Dahlgren play on the NU volleyball team?

473 Q: Who was basketball's Big Eight player of the year in 1981?

474 Q: Who ranks as the all-time assist leader for the NU men's basketball team?

475 Q: Name the Husker women's golfer who qualified for the U.S. Amateur Championships in 1994.

476 Q: Who was the first Afro-American athlete in NU history?

477 Q: From what Nebraska city was Ed Weir recruited?

478 Q: What NU football player's grandmother lived across the street from Irving Fryar's parents in New Jersey?

479 Q: Who started at quarterback for Tom Osborne's first NU team?

480 Q: What NFL team drafted Johnny Rodgers?

481 Q: Who was the leading receiver in the 1995 Orange Bowl?

482 Q: Name the member of the NU women's cross country team who was honored as an All-American in 1993-94.

483 Q: Who caught the only NU touchdown pass in the 1995 Orange Bowl?

484 Q: What does the "I" stand for in the former Husker I.M. Hipp's name?

485 Q: Who led the Huskers in tackles during the 1995 Orange Bowl?

486 Q: In what year did Husker male gymnast Tom Schlesinger win the "Today's Top Eight" award?

487 Q: What was the only college football team to intercept a Tommie Frazier pass in the 1992 season?

473 A: NU's Andre Smith

474 A: Brian Carr

475 A: Heidi Wall

476 A: George Flippin

477 A: Superior, NE

478 A: Mike Rozier

479 A: Steve Runty

480 A: San Diego Chargers

481 A: Abdul Muhammad with four catches and 60 yards

482 A: Theresa Stelling

483 A: Tight end Mark Gilman

484 A: Isaiah

485 A: Barron Miles had 9 tackles.

486 A: 1989

487 A: Oklahoma

488 Q: What position did Husker quarterback Turner Gill play on the NU baseball team?

489 Q: What position was NU's Turner Gill recruited to play professionally?

490 Q: Name the two NFL teams that Husker quarterback for whom Jerry Tagge played.

491 Q: Name one of the two Husker male gymnasts who were presented with "Today's Top Eight" award.

492 Q: Fullback Mark Schellen played for what college prior to walking on at the University of Nebraska?

493 Q: Who was Tom Osborne's first I-back?

494 Q: Which Nebraska All-American changed positions to go head-to-head against Miami's Warren Sapp in the 1995 Orange Bowl?

495 Q: Who was the last Nebraska fullback to lead the team in rushing yardage?

496 Q: Who was the team rushing leader in the 1970 championship season?

497 Q: Which running back led the Huskers in total rushing yards in both 1974 and 1975?

498 Q: At which school did Jarvis Redwine start his collegiate football career?

499 Q: How many members of the 1994 men's gymnastic team at Nebraska were named to the Phillips 66 Academic Honor Roll?

500 Q: Whose career scoring record did Mike Rozier break at Nebraska?

501 Q: What was significant about the two leading rushers in the Big Eight in 1992?

488 A: Shortstop

489 A: Shortstop for the Chicago White Sox

490 A: Green Bay and Chicago

491 A: Tom Schlesinger and Patrick Kirksey

492 A: University of Nebraska/Omaha

493 A: Tony Davis

494 A: Right guard Brendon Stai

495 A: Tony Davis in 1973

496 A: Joe Orduna with 834 yards

497 A: Monte Anthony

498 A: Oregon State

499 A: Six

500 A: Johnny Rodgers

501 A: Derek Brown and Calvin Jones both played for Nebraska.

502 Q: How many career touchdown receptions did Husker great Johnny Rodgers collect?

503 Q: The arrival of which quarterback forced Frank Patrick to move to a new position in 1969?

504 Q: Who was the last Husker to have more than 30 pass receptions in one season?

505 Q: Which Nebraska tight end eventually became a state senator?

506 Q: Which Husker hit the first home run in Buck Beltzer Stadium?

507 Q: Which Husker lineman went by the name of "Big Ed" during his Nebraska days?

508 Q: Who was the defensive coordinator for the Husker football team from 1982-93?

509 Q: What Husker linebacker was also the Big Eight discus champion in 1978?

510 Q: Name the Husker who had 71 unassisted tackles in 1970.

511 Q: What NU pitcher threw the first perfect game in Buck Beltzer Stadium?

512 Q: Who was the Big Eight quarterback that thrashed the NU secondary throwing for 489 yards against the Huskers in a 1993 conference battle?

513 Q: Which NU football player carried the nickname "Big Fig"?

514 Q: Which Husker had the most quarterback sacks during the 1995 Orange Bowl?

502 A: 26

503 A: Jerry Tagge

504 A: Johnny Mitchell caught 31 passes in 1991.

505 A: Jim McFarland

506 A: Mark Haley

507 A: "Big" Ed Weir

508 A: Charlie McBride

509 A: Lee Kunz

510 A: Jerry Murtaugh

511 A: Cliff Faust

512 A: Chad May from Kansas State

513 A: All-American tackle Bob Newton

514 A: Dwayne Harris with 3

515 Q: What nickname was given to tight end Jamie Williams during his Nebraska playing days?

516 Q: Which Husker was nicknamed "The Prince"?

517 Q: How many seniors did the Husker women's basketball team have in the 1994-95 season?

518 Q: Which Husker great was named to the nation's All-American Centennial Team?

519 Q: Who was the first All-American ball carrier for Nebraska?

520 Q: Who was NU's first All-American under the leadership of Bob Devaney?

521 Q: Who was the only Husker selected in the first round of the NFL draft in 1973?

522 Q: Who is NU's career leader in 3-point shooting for the men's basketball team?

523 Q: Who was the only player selected in the first round of the NFL draft in 1994?

524 Q: Who was the first African-American football athlete at NU to be named a team captain for an entire season?

525 Q: Which football player was named Big Eight Defensive Player of the Year in 1993?

526 Q: Who led the Husker baseball team in home runs in 1994?

527 Q: Who was the last NU pitcher to hurl a no-hitter for the Huskers?

528 Q: What two sports did Erick Strickland play while at NU?

529 Q: Who was the last All-American Husker in 1952 prior to the Devaney era?

515 A: "The Iceman"

516 A: Vince Ferragamo

517 A: Zero

518 A: Ed Weir was named as tackle in 1969.

519 A: Guy Chamberlain in 1915

520 A: Bob Brown was named All-American as a guard in 1963.

521 A: Johnny Rodgers

522 A: Eric Piatkowski

523 A: Trev Alberts

524 A: Bill Thornton

525 A: Trev Alberts

526 A: Darin Erstad with 12

527 A: Joe Giordinella in 1985

528 A: Baseball and Basketball

529 A: Jerry Minnick

530 Q: Which 1975 Husker football player later became a team physician for the Nebraska football program?

531 Q: Who was the first Husker All-Big Eight running back?

532 Q: Which Nebraska Football player was selected in the first round of the NFL draft in 1983?

533 Q: Who was the Clemson athlete who boasted that he would handle Dave Rimington in the 1982 Orange Bowl but instead ended up without a single tackle?

534 Q: Who was the NU quarterback in the loss of the 1982 Orange Bowl?

535 Q: With what professional baseball program did Erick Strickland play?

536 Q: Who was the quarterback that helped Kansas State shut out the Huskers 12-0 in 1968?

537 Q: What was the Huskers old nemesis Thomas Lott's physical trademark?

538 Q: What Oklahoma back led the Sooners to a 47-0 romp over the Huskers in 1968?

539 Q: Which NU basketball center gave football a try in 1987?

540 Q: What freshman pitcher hurled the last no-hitter recorded by the NU baseball team?

541 Q: Which Husker intercepted Frank Costa's pass to end Miami's final chance to score in the 1995 Orange Bowl?

542 Q: Which NU football player was the first to lead the Big Eight in scoring as both a freshman and a sophomore?

543 Q: In what year did Omahan Dave Hoppen join the Husker basketball team?

530 A: Tom Heiser

531 A: Bill Thornton in 1961

532 A: Dave Rimington

533 A: William "Refrigerator" Perry

534 A: Mark Mauer who took over for an injured Turner Gill

535 A: The Florida Marlins

536 A: Lynn Dickey

537 A: He wore a bandanna under his helmet.

538 A: Steve Owens who went on to win the Heisman in 1969

539 A: Keith Neubert played tight end for the Huskers.

540 A: Anthony Kelly

541 A: Kareem Moss

542 A: Calvin Jones

543 A: 1982

544 Q: Who are the four NU All-American quarterbacks from the Devaney/Osborne era?

545 Q: Name the Husker wingback who also set the school long jump record in 1985.

546 Q: Which Husker won the All-Around competition in the 1994 NCAA Men's Gymnastics Championships?

547 Q: Name the I-back who made All-Big Eight in 1984 and only started in one game for the Huskers.

548 Q: Who was Nebraska's smallest football player in 1965?

549 Q: Name the future Dallas Cowboy who was tackled at the 5-yard line on the last play of a NU victory over Oklahoma State in 1965.

550 Q: What number did the Husker center Dave Hoppen wear for NU?

551 Q: What NU back was chastised for taunting the Sooners by back pedaling the final 5 yards of an 89 yard touchdown run against Oklahoma in 1980?

552 Q: Name the Penn State quarterback that engineered the final scoring drive to defeat Nebraska in 1982?

553 Q: Name the female gymnast from NU to become the school's first individual event national champion?

554 Q: Which Husker back from the mid-1980's went on to star with the Kansas City Chiefs and Tampa Bay Buccaneers in the NFL?

555 Q: Name the Husker third string quarterback in 1977 that later earned a job with the NFL New Orleans Saints.

556 Q: From which city in Indiana was Husker basketball great Jack Moore recruited?

544 A: Jerry Tagge, Dave Humm, Vince Ferragamo and Steve Taylor

545 A: Von Sheppard

546 A: Dennis Harrison

547 A: Doug DuBose

548 A: Frank Solich at 162 pounds

549 A: Walt Garrison

550 A: 42

551 A: Jarvis Redwine

552 A: Todd Blackledge

553 A: Michele Bryant

554 A: Jeff Smith

555 A: Ed Burns

556 A: Muncie, IN

557 Q: Name the Husker from the late 1960's who played high school football for Boys Town, collegiately at NU and professionally for Los Angeles and Seattle.

558 Q: From what Nebraska city was Dale Klein recruited?

559 Q: Name the Husker defensive tackle chosen in the first-round of the NFL draft by the Dallas Cowboys.

560 Q: Who are the only two Husker tight ends to be chosen in the first round of the NFL draft?

561 Q: Which former Husker was the only men's gymnast in the 1992 Olympics to win a Gold Medal?

562 Q: Which two Nebraska basketball players were each named twice as Jack Moore Award winners?

563 Q: Who was the MVP of the 1987 Sugar Bowl?

564 Q: Who carried the nickname "Slick" during his Nebraska days?

565 Q: What was Trev Alberts' number?

566 Q: What was quarterback Steve Taylor's number?

567 Q: What NU great broke his leg in a game against Iowa State in 1964?

568 Q: What brand of bat do the majority of Husker baseball players use?

569 Q: Which Nebraska player placed third in the Heisman voting in 1972?

570 Q: Which Nebraska player was in the running for the Outland Trophy and the Heisman Trophy in 1972?

571 Q: Why did NU sprinter, Charlie Green, wear sunglasses when he ran a race?

557 A: Ken Geddes

558 A: Seward, NE

559 A: Danny Noonan

560 A: Junior Miller and Johnny Mitchell

561 A: Trent Dimas

562 A: Dave Hoppen and Eric Piatkowski

563 A: Steve Taylor

564 A: Anthony Steels

565 A: 34

566 A: 9

567 A: Quarterback Fred Duda

568 A: Easton

569 A: Rich Glover

570 A: Rich Glover

571 A: He did not want the opposition to see the fear in his eyes.

572 Q: Who was Nebraska's first, first-round NFL draft choice?

573 Q: Which Husker was the MVP of the 1985 Sugar Bowl?

574 Q: Who was the first NU player to be the first player picked in the NFL draft?

575 Q: Name the NU defensive back who was also the first Nebraska prep athlete to clear 14 feet in the pole vault.

576 Q: What two great backs from the 1960's came to Nebraska from West Bend, Wisconsin?

577 Q: Name the Husker who won the only mens gymnastics gold medal for the U.S. in the 1992 Olympics.

578 Q: Name the two offensive linemen who wrestled for the 1982 Nebraska Class A heavyweight title.

579 Q: Which Husker was named MVP of the 1992 Coca-Cola Bowl in Tokyo?

580 Q: Who scored the touchdown that enabled USC to tie the game in the 1970 Nebraska/USC game?

581 Q: What NU basketball athlete is nicknamed the "Rubber Band Man"?

582 Q: Who was the NU back that rushed for 113 yards in Osborne's first victory over Oklahoma?

583 Q: Whose 17 yard touchdown run provided the winning score for the Huskers in the victory over Oklahoma in 1983?

584 Q: What number did Husker Monte Anthony wear?

585 Q: His 64 yard run for a touchdown against UCLA in 1984 was his first score as a Husker. Name this back.

586 Q: Which Husker basketball player was the first to be chosen all-conference three times?

572 A: Lloyd Cardwell was chosen by Detroit in 1937.

573 A: Craig Sundberg

574 A: Irving Fryar by New England in 1984

575 A: Randy Reeves

576 A: Dan Schneiss and Ron Kirkland

577 A: Trent Dimas

578 A: John McCormick and Stan Parker

579 A: Tommie Frazier

580 A: Clarence Davis

581 A: Mikkie Moore

582 A: Rick Berns

583 A: Mark Schellen

584 A: 49

585 A: Doug DuBose

586 A: Jerry Fort

587 Q: Broderick Thomas was recruited from which city?

588 Q: Name the Husker athlete that went to the Super Bowl in his rookie season with the Los Angeles Rams.

589 Q: Which Husker was chosen in the third round of the NFL draft by the San Francisco 49ers in 1985?

590 Q: Who was Nebraska's starting quarterback for the 1973 Orange Bowl game?

591 Q: Which Husker basketball player was a two-time All-Big Eight selection in 1966-67 and 1967-68?

592 Q: Name the Miami player who knocked away the Turner Gill 2 point conversion   pass to preserve the Hurricane victory in the 1984 Orange Bowl.

593 Q: Who had a 19-yard run on a fumbleroosky play for Nebraska in the 1984 Orange Bowl?

594 Q: Which Husker rushed for 147 yards in the 1984 Orange Bowl?

595 Q: Whose extra point kick proved to be the winning margin in the 1983 Orange Bowl victory over LSU?

596 Q: Who scored Nebraska's only touchdown in a 34-7 loss to Tulane in the 1955 Orange Bowl?

597 Q: Name the Husker who broke away on a 77-yard punt return for a touchdown in the 1972 Orange Bowl game?

598 Q: Who was NU's first lifter of the year in 1974?

599 Q: Name one of the two captains for the 1971 Husker football team.

600 Q: What number did Husker Marc Munford wear?

601 Q: What number did Husker Bob Brown wear for Nebraska?

587 A: Houston, Texas

588 A: George Andrews

589 A: Tom Rathman

590 A: Dave Humm

591 A: Stu Lantz

592 A: Jeff Calhoun

593 A: Dean Steinkuhler

594 A: Mike Rozier

595 A: Kevin Seibel

596 A: Donald Comstock

597 A: Johnny Rodgers

598 A: Rik Bonness

599 A: Jerry Tagge and Jim Anderson

600 A: 41

601 A: 61

602 Q: Which NU men's basketball player led the Huskers in scoring and rebounding in 1966-67 and 1967-68 as a guard?

603 Q: What number did Husker Bill Thornton wear for NU?

604 Q: What did Mike Rozier and Bill Thornton have in common at Nebraska?

605 Q: From what city in Nebraska was Dean Steinkuhler recruited?

606 Q: From what city in Nebraska was Husker basketball great Milton "Bus" Whitehead?

607 Q: From what eastern state was Rich Glover recruited?

608 Q: Who had the nickname of "Bus" with the men's basketball team at Nebraska?

609 Q: From what Rocky Mountain town was Rod Smith recruited?

610 Q: Which Husker quarterback carried the nickname of "The Dealer"?

611 Q: Who was nicknamed "Light Horse" in his Husker playing days?

612 Q: How many points per game did Don Maclay lead the Big Six with in the 1930 season: 6.5, 9, 11.2 or 15?

613 Q: Who carried the nickname of "The Fly" during his NU days?

614 Q: Why didn't Vince Ferragamo play in the 1975 season opener against Louisiana State?

615 Q: From what city in Nebraska was Monte Anthony recruited?

616 Q: Which NU quarterback led the Huskers to a 1978 win over Oklahoma?

602 A: Stu Lantz

603 A: 30

604 A: They both wore No. 30.

605 A: Burr, NE

606 A: Scottsbluff

607 A: New Jersey

608 A: Milton "Bus" Whitehead

609 A: Thornton, CO

610 A: Dave Humm

611 A: Harry Wilson

612 A: 11.2 points

613 A: Guy Ingles

614 A: He was on a one game suspension for an NCAA rule violation.

615 A: Bellevue, NE

616 A: Tom Sorely

617 Q: Kansas had less total rushing yards than what NU back in 1992?

618 Q: Name the only Nebraska football player from 1917 who was also a band member.

619 Q: From what town in Pennsylvania was Ben Gregory recruited?

620 Q: With what team did Turner Gill play professional football?

621 Q: From which school did Vince Ferragamo transfer to Nebraska?

622 Q: Which Husker walk-on set a school record for rushing yards in a single season by a fullback?

623 Q: Which NU running back's single game rushing yards record was broken when Rick Berns rushed for 255 yards against Missouri?

624 Q: What number did Irving Fryar wear for Nebraska?

625 Q: Who was nicknamed "The Fig" in his Husker playing days?

626 Q: What position did Mike Stigge play with the Nebraska football team?

627 Q: From what western state was Dave Humm recruited?

628 Q: What two Husker quarterbacks were alternated during the 1969 season?

629 Q: What position did All-American Karen Dahlgren play on the NU volleyball team?

630 Q: What position did All-American Val Novak play on the NU volleyball team?

617 A: Calvin Jones

618 A: Ed Lanphere

619 A: Uniontown

620 A: The Montreal Concordes

621 A: University of California

622 A: Tom Rathman

623 A: I.M. Hipp's 254 yard record

624 A: 27

625 A: Bob Newton

626 A: Punter

627 A: Nevada

628 A: Jerry Tagge and Van Brownson

629 A: Middle Blocker

630 A: Setter

631 Q: What position did All-American great Guy Chamberlain play for the Huskers?

632 Q: What number did Jeff Kinney wear at Nebraska?

633 Q: What position did All-American great Bob Brown play for the Nebraska football team?

634 Q: What number did Husker great Bob Brown wear for Nebraska?

635 Q: What Nebraska old-timer had the nickname of "Blue"?

636 Q: What number did All-Big Seven center Bus Whitehead wear for the Huskers?

637 Q: What position did Pat Fischer play at Nebraska?

638 Q: What number did Husker great Pat Fischer wear for Nebraska?

639 Q: Name one of the four All-Americans for the NU men's basketball team from the 1930's.

640 Q: How did defender Jim Pillen make the headlines in the 1978 football season?

641 Q: Who carried the nickname of "Thunder" for the Husker football team?

642 Q: Who was known as "Twinkle Toes" on the Huskers football team?

643 Q: Which NU football player had "The Leg" for a nickname?

644 Q: Who is the only NU fullback to rush for over 200 yards in one game?

645 Q: Name the Husker also known as the "Tecumseh Tornado."

631 A: End

632 A: 35

633 A: Offensive Guard

634 A: 64

635 A: Edward E. Howell

636 A: 14

637 A: Halfback

638 A: 40

639 A: Don Maclay, Steve Hokuf, George Wahlquist and Robert Parsons

640 A: He fell on the Billy Sims fumble at the end of the OU game.

641 A: Bill "Thunder" Thornton

642 A: Jim Baffico

643 A: Craig Johnson

644 A: Frank Solich rushed for 204 yards in 1965.

645 A: Tony Davis

646 Q: What Husker was nicknamed "No Pain" at Nebraska?

647 Q: Which Husker was nicknamed the "Mosquito" at NU?

648 Q: Who was the last three-time all-conference player for the Husker's football team?

649 Q: What number did Jerry Murtaugh wear for the Huskers?

650 Q: Name one of the two Huskers chosen in the first round of the 1964 NFL draft.

651 Q: Who was the first recipient of the Guy Chamberlain Trophy?

652 Q: Who at Nebraska went by the nickname of "Doc" ?

653 Q: Name one of the two tight ends from Nebraska that were chosen in the first round of the NFL draft.

654 Q: Only two I-backs have been named "Lifter of the Year" at Nebraska. Name one of them.

655 Q: Who was the great quarterback for LSU that the Huskers faced in the 1971 Orange Bowl?

656 Q: Which Husker from the 1920's was nicknamed "Choppy"?

657 Q: Who was known as "Champ" at Nebraska?

658 Q: What was "Vike" Francis' real name?

659 Q: Who was Nebraska's first player in the Hula Bowl?

660 Q: Which Husker was nicknamed the "Big Moose" in the 1920's?

661 Q: Name two of the three Huskers that were chosen in the first round of the 1984 NFL draft.

662 Q: Who was the first recipient of the Tom Novak Award?

646 A: Wayne Meylan

647 A: Chuck Malito

648 A: Will Shields

649 A: 42

650 A: Bob Brown and Lloyd Voss

651 A: Marv Mueller in 1967

652 A: E.J. "Doc" Stewart

653 A: Junior Miller and Johnny Mitchell

654 A: I.M. Hipp and Jeff Smith

655 A: Bert Jones

656 A: John "Choppy" Rhodes

657 A: Guy "Champ" Chamberlain

658 A: Viscount Francis

659 A: Kent McCloughan

660 A: Dave the "Big Moose" Noble

661 A: Mike Rozier, Dean Steinkuhler and Irving Fryar

662 A: Charles Toogood in 1950

663 Q: Name one of the two players chosen in the first round of the 1991 NFL draft.

664 Q: Which Husker had the nickname "Link" during his playing days?

665 Q: Which Husker scored the winning points in the victory over Florida at the 1974 Sugar Bowl?

666 Q: Who came off the bench to lead the Huskers to a 1977 Liberty bowl victory?

667 Q: What number did Jack Moore wear for the Husker basketball team?

668 Q: Within one inch, how tall was Husker basketball great Jack Moore?

669 Q: Who was named "Dollar Bill" at Nebraska?

670 Q: Who came in off the bench to replace Dave Humm to help win the 1974 Sugar Bowl?

671 Q: What Florida State Quarterback burned the Huskers with 422 yards passing and 5 touchdowns in the 1990 Fiesta Bowl?

672 Q: What quarterback burned Nebraska's defense and led Alabama to a 34-7 Sugar bowl victory in 1967?

673 Q: Name the Husker who was also known as "Slick."

674 Q: Which Colorado running back gave Nebraska fits in the 1970 championship season?

675 Q: Name the only Husker taken in the first round of the 1989 NFL draft.

676 Q: What famous quarterback from Kansas State did the Blackshirts intercept seven times in the 1970 season?

663 A: Bruce Pickens and Mike Croel

664 A: William R. "Link" Lyman

665 A: Kicker Mike Coyle

666 A: Quarterback Randy Garcia

667 A: 14

668 A: 5'9"

669 A: "Dollar" Bill Bryant

670 A: Terry Luck

671 A: Peter Tom Willis

672 A: Kenny Stabler

673 A: Anthony Steels

674 A: Cliff Branch

675 A: Broderick Thomas

676 A: Lynn Dickey

677 Q: What Husker was injured in the 1982 Missouri game, creating a big controversy and almost caused NU to lose the contest?

678 Q: Who had the nickname "Mad Dog" at Nebraska?

679 Q: Who continued to play in the 1974 Wisconsin game after suffering a broken jaw?

680 Q: When was every member of the NU football team made an Admiral of the Nebraska Navy?

681 Q: What was the first father and son combination to both letter in the sport of football for Nebraska?

682 Q: Who was the only Husker chosen in the first round of the 1975 NFL draft?

683 Q: Name the three Huskers who went on to win Super Bowl XXIV rings with the San Francisco 49ers.

684 Q: How was Dave Hoppen's basketball career ended?

685 Q: What position did Erick Strickland play for the NU basketball team?

686 Q: What former Husker tied two NFL records in his rookie season by returning two kickoffs in one game for 92 and 98 yards?

687 Q: What former Husker quarterback is quoted as stating, "I'm a Buffalo fan until they play Nebraska?

688 Q: What was Husker great, Neil Smith's number?

689 Q: What NU pitcher recorded the first shut-out in Buck Beltzer Stadium?

690 Q: What was Husker great gymnast Scott Johnson's first year at Nebraska?

677 A: Turner Gill was shoved to the ground and received a concussion.

678 A: Jack Hazen

679 A: John O'Leary

680 A: After breaking OU's 75 game unbeaten streak in 1959

681 A: Grove and Morton Porter

682 A: Tom Ruud

683 A: Roger Craig, Tom Rathman and Jamie Williams

684 A: A knee injury

685 A: Guard

686 A: Tyrone Hughes with the New Orleans Saints

687 A: Bob Churchich

688 A: 99

689 A: Tim Burke

690 A: 1980

691 Q: In what year did Husker male gymnast Patrick Kirksey earn the "Today's Top Eight" award?

692 Q: Who was the winner of the Dr. Tom Heiser Award in 1994?

693 Q: Which Husker won the 1994 women's basketball Iron Woman Award?

694 Q: Name the Football Lifter -of-the-Year award winner in 1994.

695 Q: What NU player placed ninth in the Heisman voting in 1967?

696 Q: Where was Johnny Rodgers when he predicted he would score 20 touchdowns in his senior season?

697 Q: Name the defensive end that graduated in 1978 who later starred with the Los Angeles Rams.

698 Q: What position did Shane Swanson play for the Husker football team?

699 Q: From what Nebraska city was safety Brett Clark recruited?

700 Q: What two sports did Jim Huge play at NU from 1960-62?

701 Q: Name the 1985 I-back who won the Big Eight indoor 60-yard dash.

702 Q: What vehicle did Monte Kiffin borrow to return from a campus party?

703 Q: What trick did Frank Solich try in order to avoid being the smallest player on the Husker football team?

691 A: 1991

692 A: John Archer

693 A: Lis Brenden

694 A: Donta Jones

695 A: Wayne Meylan

696 A: From a wheelchair in Methodist Hospital in Omaha

697 A: George Andrews

698 A: Wingback

699 A: Nebraska City, NE

700 A: Basketball and football

701 A: Keith Jones

702 A: A milk truck

703 A: He taped a 5 pound weight to his pants during weigh-ins.

689 Q: What NU pitcher recorded the first shut-out in Buck Beltzer Stadium?

2. Coaches

754 Q: What was the first bowl game that Bob Devaney coached for the Huskers?

704 Q: Who was the first football coach in NU history?

705 Q: Who won the Big Eight coach-of-the-year award in men's basketball after the 1979-80 season?

706 Q: Who are the only active coaches posting more career victories in 1994 than Tom Osborne?

707 Q: What famous collegiate football coach turned down a job offer to coach the 1925 Cornhuskers?

708 Q: What position does Bob Devaney presently hold at the University?

709 Q: How many Big Eight titles has Terry Pettit won with the women's volleyball team: 5, 12, 17, or 20?

710 Q: Who coached NU's football team to its most consecutive victories?

711 Q: Who is the only man to coach the Huskers' football team on two separate occasions?

712 Q: How many consecutive losses did Bob Devaney experience as a head coach?

713 Q: How many times was Bob Devaney named Big Eight coach-of- the-year?

714 Q: Which member of the Cornhusker staff ended a 42 year career following the 1995 Orange Bowl?

715 Q: Who has coached the most games for the NU men's basketball team?

716 Q: What was the name of the conference NU competed in when football coach D.X. Bible's Huskers won six titles?

717 Q: Which Nebraska football coach had the best career winning percentage?

704 A: Dr. Landon Frothingham

705 A: It was shared by Joe Cipriano and Moe Iba of NU.

706 A: Joe Paterno and Bobby Bowden

707 A: Knute Rockne

708 A: Athletic Director Emeritus

709 A: 17

710 A: Walter C. "Bummy" Booth

711 A: George Clark in 1945 and again in 1948

712 A: Two consecutive losses on four separate occasions

713 A: Five times

714 A: Head Athletics Trainer, George Sullivan

715 A: Joe Cipriano

716 A: The Big Six

717 A: E.O. "Jumbo" Stiehm with a record of 35-2-3

718 Q: Where was NU's football coach Bill Glassford's pre-season training camp held?

719 Q: What team gave both Bob Devaney and Tom Osborne their first loss as head coach of the Huskers?

720 Q: Which Husker football coach was nicknamed "The Little Colonel"?

721 Q: At how many schools was Husker Baseball Coach John Sanders the head coach prior to joining Nebraska?

722 Q: What three Husker football coaches were also former athletes on the team?

723 Q: Where did Bob Devaney play collegiate football?

724 Q: Who was the NU Athletic Director when Bob Devaney was hired?

725 Q: How many of their 15 games did Jumbo Stiehm's first NU basketball team win?

726 Q: Which team during Bob Devaney's coaching career defeated the Huskers but ended up with a losing season?

727 Q: Who was named the Omaha World Herald College Athlete of the Year in 1959?

728 Q: Where was Turner Gill an assistant coach prior to returning to NU?

729 Q: Of which city in Nebraska is baseball coach John Sanders a native?

730 Q: How many tries did it take for Tom Osborne to beat the Sooners of Oklahoma?

731 Q: When Tom Osborne and Lou Holtz met on the gridiron in 1973, what university ended up the loser?

718 A: Curtis, Nebraska

719 A: University of Missouri

720 A: D.X. Bible

721 A: Two; Chemeketa Community College and Arizona Western

722 A: Glenn Presnell, A.J. Lewandowski and Bernie Masterson

723 A: Alma College in Michigan

724 A: Tippy Dye

725 A: 14

726 A: Kansas State University in 1968

727 A: Tom Osborne of Hastings College

728 A: Southern Methodist University

729 A: Grand Island

730 A: Osborne finally won on his sixth try in 1978.

731 A: North Carolina State University

732 Q: How long did Bob Devaney serve as Athletic Director of NU?

733 Q: When was the first time Tom Osborne won the Big Eight championship outright?

734 Q: How old was Tom Osborne when he took over as head coach of the Huskers?

735 Q: What Florida University tried to recruit Bob Devaney away after his 1963 season with the Huskers?

736 Q: Which Husker coach was the High School Athlete of the Year at Grand Island High School in 1964?

737 Q: Which two schools are the only opponents to shut out an Osborne-coached Nebraska team?

738 Q: What team ended Tom Osborne's 22 game win streak in 1984?

739 Q: What former Nebraska back defeated the Huskers as the head coach of the University of Missouri?

740 Q: In Bob Devaney's last year as head football coach, who was the leading rusher on the team?

741 Q: Who was NU's baseball coach prior to John Sanders?

742 Q: How many NCAA rushing titles have the Huskers won under the direction of Tom Osborne?

743 Q: What is the name of Tom Osborne's basic offensive philosophy?

744 Q: How many winning seasons did Jerry Bush lead the men's basketball team to in his 9 years as the Huskers coach?

745 Q: In what year did Tom Osborne move to the "Triple Option" offense?

732 A: 25 years

733 A: 1981

734 A: 34 years old

735 A: The Miami Hurricanes

736 A: Baseball coach John Sanders

737 A: Oklahoma and Miami

738 A: Miami Hurricanes

739 A: Warren Powers

740 A: Gary Dixon led the team with only 508 yards.

741 A: Tony Sharpe

742 A: Through 1994 Nebraska has claimed nine rushing titles.

743 A: Triple Option

744 A: Zero

745 A: 1980

746 Q: Nebraska's Fumbleroosky play was used against Oklahoma in 1979. When was the next time the Huskers used this play?

747 Q: In what year did Bob Devaney change the offensive philosophy to the "I-formation"?

748 Q: In what year did Terry Pettit begin coaching the NU volleyball team?

749 Q: In what year did the Husker football team first use the Bummeroosky play?

750 Q: Who in NU football history went by the name of "Bummy"?

751 Q: What did the D.X. stand for in Nebraska's football coach D.X. Bible's name?

752 Q: How many Nebraska football coaches have been inducted into the National Football Hall of Fame?

753 Q: How many times has volleyball coach Terry Pettit been named AVCA National coach of the year?

754 Q: What was the first bowl game that Bob Devaney coached for the Huskers?

755 Q: How many gymnastics coaches have won more NCAA Championships than Nebraska's Francis Allen?

756 Q: How many coaches have taken a Husker team to a bowl game?

757 Q: What bowl game was Tom Osborne's first as the NU Head Coach?

758 Q: How many bowl games did Bob Devaney coach for the Huskers?

759 Q: What is the name of the assistant volleyball coach who was a member of the United States National Team?

746 A: In the 1984 Orange Bowl

747 A: 1969

748 A: 1977

749 A: 1975 against Missouri

750 A: Head Coach Walter C. Booth

751 A: Dana Xenophon

752 A: Five including; Fielding Yost, D.X. Bible, Biff Jones, E.N. Robinson and Bob Devaney

753 A: Two times: 1986 and 1994

754 A: The 1962 Gotham Bowl

755 A: One: Gene Wettstone of Penn State

756 A: Four: Biff Jones, Bill Glassford, Bob Devaney and Tom Osborne

757 A: The 1974 Cotton Bowl against Texas

758 A: Nine

759 A: Cathy Noth

760 Q: What year was the last time Barry Switzer and Tom Osborne faced each other on the football field?

761 Q: Before the NU and Iowa football teams renewed their rivalry in 1979, what year was the last time these two met on the field?

762 Q: Who was NU's first opponent after Devaney took over as the Huskers head coach?

763 Q: Who was the Big Eight Coach-of the-Year for women's cross country in 1993-94?

764 Q: With only one National Championship, how do Tom Osborne's Huskers rank in a composite AP poll throughout his career?

765 Q: Who is the former Husker volleyball player now coaching at the University of Kansas?

766 Q: How many Athletic Directors has the University had?

767 Q: Which two opponents did the Huskers have constant trouble with during D.X. Bible's reign as head coach?

768 Q: What was the Huskers' first non-conference loss under Bob Devaney's leadership?

769 Q: When did Bob Devaney become NU's Athletic Director?

770 Q: With what Omaha high school is All-American Husker volleyball player Val Novak now coaching?

771 Q: Name the two teams that were fortunate enough to tie a Devaney coached Husker team.

772 Q: With which school did NU's football assistant Jerry Moore take a head coaching position in 1979?

773 Q: Which Husker football coach produced NU's first All-Americans?

760 A: In 1988

761 A: 1946

762 A: Division 1-AA South Dakota

763 A: NU's Jay Dirksen

764 A: Although they have just one championship, the Huskers still rank number one.

765 A: Karen Dahlgren

766 A: Eleven, dating back to 1928

767 A: Minnesota and Pittsburgh combined for a 10-0 record against NU.

768 A: A 17-13 defeat by the Air Force Academy in 1963

769 A: 1967

770 A: Westside High School

771 A: Southern California and Iowa State

772 A: North Texas State

773 A: "Jumbo" Stiehm coached Vic Halligan in 1914 and Guy Chamberlin in 1915.

774 Q: In what three consecutive seasons did the NU football team lose their opening games under Tom Osborne's direction?

775 Q: When was the only time Tom Osborne was defeated by a team that ended the season with a losing record?

776 Q: Name the two sports NU football assistant George Darlington played at Rutgers University.

777 Q: How many times did a Devaney-coached Husker team gain over 400 yards rushing?

778 Q: How many times have the Osborne-coached Huskers lost when rushing for 400 or more yards?

779 Q: What was the Huskers largest margin of defeat under the direction of Bob Devaney?

780 Q: From which university in Colorado did Husker baseball coach John Sanders graduate?

781 Q: Who is the only assistant from Tom Osborne's original staff still remaining?

782 Q: How many times under Tom Osborne have the Huskers been defeated in their last two games of the season?

783 Q: In what city did Tom Osborne attend grade school?

784 Q: How many years did Bob Devaney coach at Wyoming?

785 Q: What was Tom Osborne's first full-time coaching job?

786 Q: Carl Selmer was a candidate for the head coaching position for the NU football team in 1973. Although he did not receive the position, where did he eventually coach?

787 Q: Where was Bob Devaney's first coaching job?

788 Q: What sport other than football has Bob Devaney coached?

774 A: 1976,1977 and 1978

775 A: Iowa State in 1992

776 A: Football and Lacrosse

777 A: Two times: 1965 and 1971

778 A: They never have.

779 A: NU was shut out 47-0 in 1968 by Oklahoma.

780 A: Northern Colorado

781 A: George Darlington

782 A: Five times and Oklahoma was a part of each one.

783 A: St. Paul, Nebraska

784 A: Five

785 A: Osborne was hired as the receivers coach at NU in 1967.

786 A: Miami

787 A: Big Beaver High School in Birmingham, Michigan

788 A: Baseball at Saginaw High School

789 Q: Bob Devaney graduated with what degree?

790 Q: What position did coach Bob Devaney play in college?

791 Q: How many children do Bob and Phyllis Devaney have?

792 Q: How many years of high school football did Bob Devaney coach?

793 Q: How many Skyline Conference titles did Devaney's Cowboys win at Wyoming?

794 Q: Who talked Bob Devaney into pursuing the NU job?

795 Q: Name the Men's tennis coach who graduated from NU in 1980.

796 Q: Which school did coach Devaney's staff visit before the 1969 season to learn more about the I-formation?

797 Q: Name the NFL team defensive coordinator for which Charlie McBride played.

798 Q: Bill Glassford played college football for this school.

799 Q: Name one of the two coaches tied for the worst winning percentage in NU football history.

800 Q: How many times has Head Coach Larry Romjue led the NU men's golf team to the national tournament?

801 Q: In five seasons, how many conference titles did E.O. "Jumbo" Stiehm win for Nebraska?

802 Q: What is E.O. Stiehm's first name?

803 Q: During his nine years with Nebraska, how many times has coach Danny Nee led the Huskers to post-season play?

804 Q: What was NU football coach D.X. Bible's nickname?

789 A: A bachelor's degree in social science

790 A: End

791 A: Two. Patricia and Michael

792 A: Fourteen

793 A: Four

794 A: Duffy Daugherty

795 A: Kerry McDermott

796 A: Southern California

797 A: The Denver Broncos

798 A: Pittsburgh

799 A: A.J. Lewandowski and A.E. Branch

800 A: Two times: 1973 and 1978

801 A: Five Missouri Valley Conference titles

802 A: Ewald

803 A: Seven times

804 A: The Little Colonel

805 Q: Why did NU football coach Bill Jennings have to be escorted by four policemen during a game at Oklahoma?

806 Q: Where did Tom Osborne sit during the game in his final year as an assistant coach with the Huskers?

807 Q: With which NFL team did Tom Osborne seriously consider coaching?

808 Q: How many times has Head Coach Francis Allen coached the Men's Olympic gymnastics team?

809 Q: What role did Tom Osborne play in Turner and Gayle Gill's wedding ceremony?

810 Q: Why did Tom Osborne once take a lie detector test?

811 Q: Name the former Husker recruiting director that joined the staff at Ohio State in 1988?

812 Q: What was Bob Devaney's first big victory on the road?

813 Q: To how many NCAA Championships has Husker Gymnastics coach Francis Allen led his athletes?

814 Q: Who was the first paid employee hired to coach the Nebraska football team?

815 Q: How many Olympians have been coached by NU's Francis Allen?

816 Q: For what university did NU gymnastics coach Francis Allen compete as an athlete?

817 Q: Which two schools are the only ones to have more NCAA men's gymnastics titles than NU?

818 Q: Who is the Huskers Sports Information Director?

819 Q: On what property is the Bob Devaney Sports Center located?

805 A: OU accused Jennings of contributing information that put Oklahoma on probation with the NCAA.

806 A: In the press box

807 A: Seattle Seahawks

808 A: Two times: 1980 and 1992

809 A: He was a groomsman.

810 A: To answer wrongful allegations of offering illegal inducements to a recruit in 1985

811 A: Steve Pederson

812 A: Beating Michigan in the second game of his first season

813 A: Eight

814 A: Frank Crawford

815 A: Four

816 A: The University of Nebraska

817 A: Illinois and Penn State

818 A: Chris Anderson

819 A: Nebraska State Fairgrounds

820 Q: What is the former Nebraska sports information director Don Bryant's nickname?

821 Q: Who is the director of the Nebraska marching band?

822 Q: How many times during the regular season has the NU men's gymnastics team gone undefeated under the coaching of Francis Allen?

823 Q: Who is the host of the Tom Osborne Show?

824 Q: When was Bob Devaney's first undefeated Big Eight season?

825 Q: Does Tom Osborne have a losing percentage against ranked opponents?

826 Q: Which 3 teams shut out the Huskers during the Devaney era?

827 Q: What was Devaney's longest undefeated streak?

828 Q: Name the Husker athlete who later became the coach of the NU football and basketball programs.

829 Q: Name the head diving coach for the Huskers.

830 Q: Name the former Husker athlete who is now the head coach of the women's basketball team at the University of Nebraska at Kearney.

831 Q: Name the Huskers' Senior Associate Athletic Director in charge of compliance.

832 Q: How many head coaches in NU school history have directed the women's track team?

833 Q: How did the coaching staff at Nebraska discover Mike Rozier?

834 Q: Which Nebraska player drew caricatures of all the coaches for the 1968 football media guide?

820 A: The Fat Fox

821 A: Jay Kloecker

822 A: Five

823 A: Kent Pavelka

824 A: 1963

825 A: No, he has a 59% winning mark.

826 A: Kansas, Kansas State and Oklahoma

827 A: Thirty-three games

828 A: E.O. "Jumbo" Stiehm

829 A: Jim Hocking

830 A: Amy Stephens

831 A: Al Papik

832 A: Three

833 A: Watching high school films of another player

834 A: Dick Davis

835 Q: What Devaney comment after the 1971 bowl games fired-up Notre Dame fans?

836 Q: Who was the first men's basketball coach for the university?

837 Q: Which NU football coach served as a decathlon coach during the 1928 Olympic Games?

838 Q: Who was the coach at Hastings College during Osborne's playing days?

839 Q: For what two professional teams did Tom Osborne play?

840 Q: Who is the only NU men's basketball coach to lead the Huskers to more victories than Danny Nee?

841 Q: Who was the last member of the original Wyoming/Bob Devaney crew to coach at Nebraska?

842 Q: Which NU head football coach was an assistant at Oklahoma for five years prior to coming to the Huskers?

843 Q: Who were Nebraska's losingest football coaches based on percentage of wins?

844 Q: Name the head coach for the Nebraska cross country team.

845 Q: Who coached the 1915 Husker football team that beat Notre Dame?

846 Q: Name the Husker who coached at Washington State University following a NFL career and now coaches at San Jose City College.

847 Q: How many Nebraska athletic directors have also been coaches for the Husker's football team?

848 Q: How many football coaches have there been in Nebraska history?

835 A: He said, "not even the Pope could vote for Notre Dame" as the number one team.

836 A: Frank Lehmer

837 A: Henry Schulte

838 A: Tom McLaughlin

839 A: Washington Redskins and San Francisco 49ers

840 A: Joe Cipriano

841 A: John Melton

842 A: Pete Elliott

843 A: A.J. Lewandowski and A.E. Branch

844 A: Jay Dirksen

845 A: E.O. "Jumbo" Stiehm

846 A: Rich Glover

847 A: Five

848 A: 28

849 Q: How many times has Devaney been a head coach of a team appearing in the Sun Bowl?

850 Q: Who is the Husker's tennis coach for the women's team?

851 Q: What is the name of the men's tennis coach for Nebraska?

852 Q: Which coach carried the nickname "Pa" in his Husker days?

853 Q: Who served as NU's track coach from 1939 to 1955?

854 Q: In what year did NU hire its first full-time strength coach?

855 Q: Name the Senior Women's Administrator for the athletic department at Nebraska.

856 Q: Name one of the three Big Six coaches in 1947 who had played for Nebraska.

857 Q: Who was the football coach for NU when the team played in their first game at Memorial Stadium?

858 Q: What was the final ranking of Bob Devaney's first Nebraska team?

859 Q: In terms of championships, who is the most successful coach at the University of Nebraska?

860 Q: How many undefeated Big Eight seasons did Bob Devaney have?

861 Q: How many undefeated Big Eight seasons did Tom Osborne have in the 1980's?

862 Q: Name the Husker's gymnastics coach for the women's team.

863 Q: How many coaches did Tom Novak play for at NU?

849 A: Two: once with Wyoming and once with Nebraska

850 A: Scott Jacobson

851 A: Kerry McDermott

852 A: Henry F. Shulte

853 A: Ed Weir

854 A: 1970

855 A: Dr. Barbara Hibner

856 A: Sam Francis, George Sauer and Bernie Masterson

857 A: Fred Dawson

858 A: They were not ranked his first year.

859 A: Men's gymnastics coach Francis Allen

860 A: Four

861 A: Four

862 A: Dan Kendig

863 A: Three

864 Q: Name one of the three sportswriters from Lincoln who helped Bob Devaney write his autobiography.

865 Q: Name the Husker's golf coach for the women's team.

866 Q: Which NU football coach in 1911 encouraged the band to participate at the games?

867 Q: What is Bob Devaney's latest autobiography titled?

868 Q: What is the name of the coach for the Husker's softball team?

869 Q: What do Tom Osborne, Michael Jordan, Danny Thomas and Mother Theresa have in common?

870 Q: What is the name of the tutoring program for Lincoln area high school students founded by Tom Osborne?

871 Q: On what side does Tom Osborne part his hair?

872 Q: What color are Danny Nee's eyes?

873 Q: How old was Bob Devaney when he got his first college head coaching job?

874 Q: Name one of the two years in the Devaney/Osborne era that the Huskers led the nation in total defense.

875 Q: How many children do Danny and Nora Nee have?

876 Q: Who was nicknamed "Indian" at Nebraska?

877 Q: Who at NU was known as "Jumbo"?

878 Q: What coach at Nebraska was nicknamed "Potsy"?

879 Q: What coach at Nebraska was best known as "Biff"?

880 Q: How did Husker coach "Jumbo" Stiehm get his nickname?

864 A: Randy York, Mike Babcock and Virgil Parker

865 A: Robin Krapfl

866 A: E.O. "Jumbo" Stiehm

867 A: Devaney, A Dynasty Remembered

868 A: Rhonda Revelle

869 A: The Father Flanagan Service to Youth Award

870 A: Husker Teammates program

871 A: The right side

872 A: Blue

873 A: 41

874 A: 1967 and 1984

875 A: Three: Janet, Kevin and Patrick

876 A: Henry F. Shulte

877 A: E.O. "Jumbo" Stiehm

878 A: George "Potsy" Clark

879 A: L. McC. "Biff" Jones

880 A: His large size

881 Q: Which NU basketball coach is responsible for almost one quarter of the total victories in the school's history?

882 Q: Who are the only All-American tight ends coached by Tom Osborne?

883 Q: What was the meaning of the "Double Hundred" celebration?

884 Q: How many different bowl games has Nebraska played in since Tom Osborne started coaching the Huskers?

885 Q: Between Bob Devaney and Bear Bryant, who had the most victories head-to-head?

886 Q: What was NU's connection to Northern Illinois' football coach when they played NU in 1989 and 1990?

887 Q: When did the NU men's basketball team hire its first full-time head coach?

888 Q: How many times has Tom Osborne's Huskers faced the Rainbows of Hawaii?

889 Q: What was the last conference title for Nebraska prior to Bob Devaney taking over as head coach?

890 Q: Before Devaney, what was the last season in which the NU football team won 9 games in a season?

891 Q: Who was the first full-time coach for the Nebraska men's basketball team?

892 Q: When was the last winning season for NU prior to Bob Devaney?

893 Q: Between the 1941 Rose Bowl game and the arrival of Bob Devaney how many winning seasons did the Huskers have?

894 Q: Who coached the Kansas basketball team in 1900 when the Huskers defeated them?

881 A: Joe Cipriano

882 A: Junior Miller and Johnny Mitchell

883 A: It honored Devaney and Osborne for each winning 100 games at Nebraska.

884 A: 8 different bowls

885 A: Bear Bryant held a one game edge.

886 A: Jerry Pettibone was a former NU assistant.

887 A: 1911

888 A: Three times

889 A: The 1940 Big Six title

890 A: 1905

891 A: E.O. "Jumbo" Stiehm

892 A: 1954

893 A: Only 3 winning seasons

894 A: Dr. James Naismith

895 Q: What former Kansas All-American was the coach for the men's basketball team at Nebraska at the end of the 1920's?

896 Q: Which NU basketball coach was dubbed the "Big Bear of the Coliseum"?

897 Q: When did NU basketball coach Moe Iba announce his resignation?

898 Q: Which NU football coach was also the athletic director in 1937?

899 Q: What present-day Big Ten school did Biff Jones defeat that D.X. Bible could not?

900 Q: The first official game under the lights at Buck Beltzer Stadium also marked what victory milestone for coach Sanders?

901 Q: When was NU wrestling coach Tim Neumann's first year at the helm for the Huskers?

902 Q: Which NU football coach once said, "You can't feed the ego of the state of Nebraska with a football team"?

903 Q: Who coached the NU men's basketball team to its first outright Missouri Valley title?

904 Q: Name one of the two coaches Bob Devaney worked under while at Michigan State.

905 Q: What was Schulte's claim to fame as a Nebraska assistant?

906 Q: After being hired as the men's basketball coach for Nebraska in 1946, he turned the fortunes of the Huskers around.

907 Q: For what famous coach did Henry Shulte play?

908 Q: At what university was Henry Schulte an All-American?

895 A: Charles T. Black

896 A: Jerry Bush

897 A: Following the first round NCAA loss to Western Kentucky in 1986

898 A: Biff Jones

899 A: Minnesota

900 A: 500th victory

901 A: 1985

902 A: Bill Jennings

903 A: Sam Waugh

904 A: Biggie Munn and Duffy Daugherty

905 A: He was a great lineman coach.

906 A: Harry Good

907 A: Fielding Yost

908 A: Michigan

909 Q: Which NU coach led the men's basketball team to its first NCAA playoff game?

910 Q: For what was Rick Berns the first running back?

911 Q: Who started the term "Blackshirts"?

912 Q: In what years was NU football coach D.X. Bible at the helm of the Cornhuskers?

913 Q: Between 1942 and 1946 how many head coaches did NU have?

914 Q: NU football coach Bernie Masterson patterned his T-formation after what NFL team?

915 Q: What NU basketball assistant shared coaching duties with Joe Cipriano in 1979-80 because Cipriano was battling cancer?

916 Q: How many times has Tom Osborne's Huskers lost to unranked teams?

917 Q: In what year did Bob Devaney publish his book, "Devaney and Friends"?

918 Q: Before coaching at Wyoming, where did Bob Devaney coach?

919 Q: In 1972, NU unexpectedly tied Iowa State 23-23. Devaney said, "we played like ....?

920 Q: How many seasons did Joe Cipriano coach the men's basketball team at Nebraska?

921 Q: What did Tom Osborne's grandfather do as an occupation?

909 A: Harry Good

910 A: Tom Osborne's first victory over Oklahoma

911 A: George Kelly

912 A: 1929-1936

913 A. Four

914 A: Chicago Bears

915 A: Moe Iba

916 A; Eleven times.

917 A: 1981

918 A: Assistant coach, Michigan State

919 A: Like a bunch of farmers at a picnic.

920 A: 17

921 A: He was a preacher.

728 Q: Where was Turner Gill an assistant coach prior to returning to NU?

3. General

956 Q: Who is the former Husker volleyball
player now playing for the U.S. National
Volleyball Team?

922 Q: How many collegiate varsity sports does NU have?

923 Q: How many Homecoming football games have the Huskers lost in school history: 3, 6, 11 or 19?

924 Q: In what year did NU football have its first undefeated season?

925 Q: Who is the current President of the University of Nebraska?

926 Q: Nebraska football suffered its first loss in what year and against whom?

927 Q: True or False, the NU athletic department receives no financial support from state funding or student fees.

928 Q: What SEC team did NU defeat in the Sun Bowl in 1969?

929 Q: In what year was NU's football team first called the Cornhuskers?

930 Q: What is the seating capacity of Buck Beltzer Stadium?

931 Q: How many first team All-Americans has the NU baseball team had?

932 Q: In 1892, what Big Ten football team gave NU its first out-of-state victory?

933 Q: How many football jerseys have been retired in NU football history: 2, 6, 9 or 15?

934 Q: What two teams in 1979 did the Huskers lose to in consecutive games by a score of 17-14?

935 Q: Nebraska Football lost just two games in the 1981-83 seasons. Which two schools defeated the Huskers?

936 Q: Who was NU's Baseball America Pre-season First-Team All-American in 1995?

922 A: 22

923 A: 19

924 A: 1890

925 A: L. Dennis Smith

926 A: 1891 vs. Doane College

927 A: True

928 A: University of Georgia

929 A: 1900

930 A: 1500

931 A: Seven

932 A: University of Illinois

933 A: 9

934 A: Oklahoma and Houston

935 A: Penn State and Miami

936 A: Darin Erstad

937 Q: What Big Eight team did Nebraska defeat in 1993 with a mere 179 yards of total offense?

938 Q: Prior to the 1996 NFL draft, how many first round draft picks has Nebraska had?

939 Q: Name three of the four positions that Tom Novak played during his Husker career.

940 Q: What NFL team selected Broderick Thomas in the first round of the 1989 draft?

941 Q: In the 1979 baseball season how many of the 49 Husker wins were shutouts?

942 Q: Within 1000 students, what is the approximate NU student enrollment?

943 Q: In how many different bowls have the Nebraska Cornhuskers competed?

944 Q: Which team did the Huskers play in their only appearance in the Astro-Bluebonnet Bowl?

945 Q: How many times have the Huskers competed in the Orange Bowl?

946 Q: How many times has the NU volleyball team had a losing season under the direction of Terry Pettit?

947 Q: What did Volleyball Monthly magazine rank the 1994 Huskers volleyball team in the pre-season poll?

948 Q: How many Astro-Bluebonnet Bowl games have the Huskers won?

949 Q: Who was the rock & roll legend featured on the 1977 Liberty Bowl program?

950 Q: How many times has Oklahoma been responsible for handing the Nebraska football team their first loss of the season?

937 A: Oklahoma

938 A: 27

939 A: Fullback, Center, Guard and Linebacker

940 A: Tampa Bay

941 A: 15

942 A: 24,000

943 A: 10 bowls including; Astro-Bluebonnet, Citrus, Cotton, Fiesta, Gotham, Liberty, Orange, Rose, Sugar and Sun Bowls

944 A: NU played Texas Tech following the 1976 season.

945 A: 15 times through 1995

946 A: Zero

947 A: Second

948 A: One with a record of (1-0)

949 A: Elvis Presley

950 A: Five times

951 Q: Why did Missouri forfeit a game to Nebraska in 1892?

952 Q: What Nebraska high school did NU volleyball All-American Allison Weston attend?

953 Q: What was the incredible defensive play made by NU's Barron Miles in the 1993 game versus Oklahoma State that allowed the Huskers to take the lead 19-13 in the fourth quarter?

954 Q: Who is the famous actor that led the Bruins of UCLA over the Huskers in 1972, snapping their 23 game winning streak?

955 Q: Prior to 1928, in what conference did the Huskers compete?

956 Q: Who is the former Husker volleyball player now playing for the U.S. National Volleyball Team?

957 Q: Where did the Huskers play their home games prior to the completion of Memorial Stadium?

958 Q: How long did Lyle Bremser broadcast Nebraska football games on the radio?

959 Q: How many jerseys have been retired by the Nebraska volleyball team?

960 Q: What is the average daily temperature at the University in Lincoln?

961 Q: How many Outland Trophy winners has NU produced?

962 Q: How many Big Eight Athletes-of-the-Year has NU had?

963 Q: What Big Eight school hosted the conference wrestling tournament in 1995?

964 Q: Where does the NU wrestling team compete at home?

951 A: The Tigers refused to play the Huskers because Nebraska had an African-American running back by the name of George Flippin.

952 A: Papillion-LaVista High School in Papillion, NE

953 A: He blocked and caught a punt in the end zone to score a touchdown.

954 A: Mark Harmon

955 A: The Missouri Valley

956 A: Lori Endicott

957 A: Old Nebraska Field

958 A: 45 years between 1939-83

959 A: Three: Lori Endicott, Cathy Noth and Karen Dahlgren

960 A: 65 degrees

961 A: Seven

962 A: Ten

963 A: Nebraska

964 A: Bob Devaney Sports Center

965 Q: Which former Husker played a role on the soap opera, "Another World"?

966 Q: What NU football good-luck charm was stolen in 1987?

967 Q: Name the star of "Gunsmoke" that gave the Husker football team a pep talk prior to the 1967 Kansas game.

968 Q: What Nebraska sports use the Bob Devaney Sports Center as their home events center?

969 Q: What did the Husker football team receive from their fans prior to the 1971 Orange Bowl game?

970 Q: Why was the 1963 NU-Oklahoma game almost canceled?

971 Q: Which NU football player hitchhiked from Washington D.C. to Nebraska to walk on the team?

972 Q: In the 1993-94 academic year how many of the 21 conference championships did the Huskers win?

973 Q: What was the original proposed name for Memorial Stadium?

974 Q: What uniform colors did the Huskers wear in their first game in Memorial Stadium?

975 Q: Name the Husker back who sang the National Anthem before an NU home game in 1980.

976 Q: Which schools are the only two among the Big Twelve to offer Men's Gymnastics?

977 Q: What was Husker great Irving Fryar's nickname to his high school friends?

978 Q: What was the seating capacity when Memorial Stadium was built?

965 A: Jim Baffico

966 A: The horseshoe that hangs over the entrance leading to the field

967 A: Ken Curtis who played Festus

968 A: Gymnastics, Wrestling and Basketball

969 A: The world's largest telegram, signed by 46,500 fans

970 A: The assassination of John F. Kennedy took place the day before the game.

971 A: Langston Coleman, who played from 1963-66

972 A: Nine

973 A: War Memorial Stadium

974 A: NU wore blue uniforms against Oklahoma.

975 A: Anthony Steels

976 A: Nebraska and Oklahoma

977 A: Whiff

978 A: 31,000

979 Q: In the first six televised games for NU football, how many did the Huskers win?

980 Q: Which is the only school in the Big Twelve that does not have a baseball team?

981 Q: When was the first night game at Memorial Stadium?

982 Q: When was the Huskers' (Cook Pavilion) indoor practice facility completed?

983 Q: The Huskers football team had not beaten Oklahoma for 17 years until which season?

984 Q: What was the name of the first football league in which Nebraska was a member?

985 Q: How many of the Big Twelve schools have a wrestling program?

986 Q: When did Nebraska change their face masks to red?

987 Q: What was the name of Nebraska's first fight song?

988 Q: Name the schools that will compete in the same division as NU in the Big Twelve.

989 Q: How many women's soccer programs will be featured in the Big Twelve conference?

990 Q: With what television network does the Big Twelve conference have a contract that will extend through 2000?

991 Q: How many Big Twelve schools offer volleyball?

992 Q: Who is the title sponsor for the Big Eight basketball tournament?

993 Q: What is the zip code for the University of Nebraska?

994 Q: What was the home of the NU men's basketball team prior to the opening of the Coliseum in 1926?

979 A: Zero

980 A: Colorado

981 A: 1986 against Florida State

982 A: 1987

983 A: 1959

984 A: The Interstate Intercollegiate Football League

985 A: Five

986 A: Before the 1982 Orange Bowl

987 A: March of the Cornhuskers written by band director Billy Quick

988 A: Iowa State, Kansas, Kansas State, Colorado and Missouri

989 A: Seven

990 A: ABC

991 A: Twelve

992 A: Phillips 66

993 A: 68588

994 A: Grant Hall

995 Q: What is the name of the Nebraska softball complex?

996 Q: Within 10,000, what is the population of the city of Lincoln, NE?

997 Q: Name the family from Nebraska City that sent four members from three generations to the Husker football team.

998 Q: What is the name of the outdoor facility for the NU track team?

999 Q: Within one million dollars, what did the Bob Devaney Sports center project cost?

1000 Q: The Vollmers, an Omaha family, have three sons named after Husker quarterbacks. Name two out of the three players names chosen by Barb and Dennis Vollmer.

1001 Q: Which school in the Big Twelve does not have a men's tennis program?

1002 Q: What is the nickname of the city, Lincoln, Nebraska?

1003 Q: What is Lincoln's historic market district called?

1004 Q: What color of ball do the tennis teams at Nebraska use?

1005 Q: What color of football do the Huskers practice with on Thursdays?

1006 Q: What is written across the top of a hurdle for the NU track team?

1007 Q: What is the name of the booster club for the men's golf team?

1008 Q: What number did Husker great Guy Chamberlin wear?

1009 Q: Which school in the Big Twelve does not have a women's tennis program?

995 A: The Nebraska Softball Complex

996 A: 200,000 people

997 A: The Porter family

998 A: Ed Weir Stadium

999 A: 13 million dollars

1000 A: Tommie, Turner and Taylor

1001 A: Kansas State

1002 A: The Star City

1003 A: The Haymarket

1004 A: Yellow

1005 A: Brown

1006 A: Nebraska

1007 A: NU Fairway Club

1008 A: Teams did not wear numbers then.

1009 A: Colorado

1010 Q: What number did Rich Glover wear for Nebraska?

1011 Q: What number did Bobby Reynolds wear for Nebraska?

1012 Q: What number did Tom Novak wear for the Huskers?

1013 Q: What number did George Sauer wear for Nebraska?

1014 Q: What number did Dean Steinkuhler wear for the Huskers?

1015 Q: To what position was Johnny Rodgers switched for the 1973 Orange Bowl?

1016 Q: Where was Johnny Rodgers when he learned that he had won the Heisman Trophy?

1017 Q: How many Big Twelve schools have men's and women's cross country and track programs?

1018 Q: What place did Nebraska's Sam Francis finish in the Heisman Trophy voting in 1936?

1019 Q: What was the last NFL team for whom Nebraska's Vince Ferragamo played?

1020 Q: What position did Irving Fryar play in high school?

1021 Q: When is the 100th year of intercollegiate competition for the Nebraska men's basketball team?

1022 Q: What physical problem did Johnny Rodgers have that frequently kept him from practicing?

1023 Q: Who did Johnny Rodgers award the game ball to after the 1972 Orange Bowl?

1024 Q: Where did Husker great Jeff Kinney come from?

1025 Q: What was Nebraska fullback Dodie Donnell's real first name?

1010 A: 79

1011 A: 12

1012 A: 60

1013 A: 25

1014 A: 71

1015 A: I-back

1016 A: At Rich Glover's home in New Jersey

1017 A: All twelve

1018 A: Second

1019 A: The Green Bay Packers

1020 A: Tight End

1021 A: 1995-96 season

1022 A: Bleeding ulcers

1023 A: Rex Lowe, who contracted Hodgkin's disease, and was confined to a wheelchair

1024 A: McCook, Nebraska

1025 A: Lafayette

1026 Q: How many players have scored over 2,000 points in their career on the NU men's basketball team?

1027 Q: Name the middle guard from North Platte, Nebraska who was one of the first NU players to letter as a freshman.

1028 Q: Name Nebraska's first academic All-American.

1029 Q: For which NFL team did Husker great Jamie Williams first play?

1030 Q: What university facility is the home of the Husker swimming and diving squads?

1031 Q: What injury kept Turner Gill from playing in the 1982 Orange Bowl?

1032 Q: Where did Dean Steinkuhler play high school football?

1033 Q: Name the Nebraska City native who starred as a safety for NU in the 1980's and then joined the Atlanta Falcons.

1034 Q: Which sportswriter is credited for naming the Nebraska team "the Cornhuskers"?

1035 Q: Former sports information director Don Bryant served at two Winter Olympic games helping with what sport?

1036 Q: When were the goal posts in Memorial Stadium torn down for the first time?

1037 Q: Who was Nebraska's first Sunshine Girl?

1038 Q: What is the name of the booster club for the Husker softball team?

1039 Q: Name the Nebraska fullback who sang for a punk rock band called "Brain Hammer" in the mid-1980's.

1040 Q: The field in Memorial Stadium runs north and south. On which side of the field do the Huskers stand during a home game?

1026 A: One: Dave Hoppen with 2,167

1027 A: Kerry Weinmaster in 1976

1028 A: Don Fricke

1029 A: The Houston Oilers

1030 A: The Bob Devaney Sports Center

1031 A: Nerve damage to his leg

1032 A: Sterling, Nebraska

1033 A: Bret Clark

1034 A: Charles "Cy" Sherman

1035 A: Figure skating

1036 A: Following the 1959 upset over Oklahoma

1037 A: Joyce Burns Thingman

1038 A: The On Deck Circle

1039 A: Micah Heibel

1040 A: The east side

1041 Q: What was Husker All-American Zach Wiegert's number?

1042 Q: With how many weight-room facilities is the Devaney Center equipped?

1043 Q: How many members of the Fischer family have played football at Nebraska?

1044 Q: Name the doctor from York, Nebraska who is credited with beginning the tradition of Husker fans wearing red.

1045 Q: How many levels are in the press box at Memorial Stadium?

1046 Q: What is the name of the Nebraska Track and Field booster club?

1047 Q: What is the name of the stadium of long time Husker rival Penn State?

1048 Q: Who was the opponent for the first televised game at Memorial Stadium?

1049 Q: For what off-the-field hobby was Husker great Shane Swanson noted?

1050 Q: What recreational sport often played on the NU campus was invented in Lincoln?

1051 Q: What number did I-back Jeff Smith wear for the Huskers?

1052 Q: What were the colors of the first NU football team?

1053 Q: What was the original nickname of the 1890 Nebraska football team?

1054 Q: What is a Bugeater?

1055 Q: What brand name of basketball does the women's basketball team use at the university?

1041 A: 72

1042 A: Two

1043 A: Six

1044 A: Dr. Dexter D. King

1045 A: Three

1046 A: The Relay Club

1047 A: Beaver Stadium

1048 A: Oregon

1049 A: Rodeoing, bull riding

1050 A: Frisbee

1051 A: 28

1052 A: Black and White

1053 A: The Old Gold Knights

1054 A: An insect eating Bull Bat found on the Nebraska prairie

1055 A: Rawlings

1056 Q: Who is NU football's loudest out-of-state rival?

1057 Q: How did Nebraska's football team beat Missouri in their first meeting?

1058 Q: What is the name of the academic center for student/athletes located in Memorial Stadium?

1059 Q: Who are the "Big Three" sports announcers on Nebraska's Football Network?

1060 Q: Who served as the Big Eight's first conference commissioner?

1061 Q: How many national championships did the Big Eight capture in the 1993-94 academic year?

1062 Q: What is the name of the indoor workout facility for the NU baseball and football teams?

1063 Q: How many days does a person have to claim a lost and found item from Memorial Stadium before it is disposed of?

1064 Q: What color are the stitches on the baseballs used by the Huskers?

1065 Q: On what level are public telephones located in Memorial Stadium?

1066 Q: The Red Cross Emergency Headquarters is located at which corner of Memorial Stadium?

1067 Q: Where should a person go if they get lost in Memorial Stadium?

1068 Q: How long has the Red Cross been keeping a watchful eye on Husker fans at Memo rial Stadium?

1069 Q: What is on the front of the ball caps worn by the Husker baseball team?

1056 A: Iowa

1057 A: Missouri forfeited.

1058 A: Boekel Center

1059 A: Gary Sadlemyer, Kent Pavelka and Jim Rose

1060 A: Reeves E. Peters

1061 A: Three: OU (baseball), OSU (wrestling), NU (men's gymnastics)

1062 A: Cook Pavilion

1063 A: Seven days

1064 A: Red

1065 A: The concourse level

1066 A: Northwest

1067 A: To the First Aid station at the southeast corner of the field

1068 A: Since 1955

1069 A: A single "N"

1070 Q: What is the official field song of the Nebraska football team?

1071 Q: How many states does Nebraska's radio network cover?

1072 Q: Where was the home of Nebraska freshman football?

1073 Q: The main campus entrance from 1892 to 1922 is located in front of which Nebraska facility?

1074 Q: What is the cost for a rental seat in Memorial Stadium?

1075 Q: Which Major League Baseball team chose Darin Erstad in the first round of the 1995 draft?

1076 Q: Who were the co-captains for the 1971 national championship football team?

1077 Q: What injury knocked Mike Rozier out of the 1984 Orange bowl game against Miami?

1078 Q: What social occurrence kept 14,306 fans away from the 1983 Orange Bowl against LSU?

1079 Q: What number did Eric Piatkowski wear for Nebraska?

1080 Q: What Omaha sportscaster was a walk-on player for the Husker football team?

1081 Q: How many undefeated Big Eight seasons did Bob Devaney have?

1082 Q: Name one of the three sportswriters from Lincoln that helped Bob Devaney write his autobiography.

1083 Q: Why didn't Vince Ferragamo play in the 1975 season opener against Louisiana State?

1084 Q: What number did Jarvis Redwine wear for the Huskers?

1070 A: The Cornhusker

1071 A: 13 states

1072 A: Shulte Fieldhouse

1073 A: Ed Weir Stadium

1074 A: $ 2.00

1075 A: California Angels

1076 A: Jerry Murtaugh and Dan Schneiss

1077 A: A bruised ankle

1078 A: Racial rioting in Miami

1079 A: 52

1080 A: John Glenn

1081 A: Four

1082 A: Randy York, Mike Babcock and Virgil Parker

1083 A: He was on a one game suspension for an NCAA rule violation.

1084 A: 12

1085 Q: What did Johnny Rodgers do following his famous punt return against Oklahoma?

1086 Q: Kansas had less total rushing yards than what NU back in 1992?

1087 Q: In what city is Big Twelve opponent Texas located?

1088 Q: In what city is Big Twelve opponent Texas A&M located?

1089 Q: In what city is Big Twelve opponent Texas Tech located?

1090 Q: Which team did NU defeat in the 1969 Sun bowl?

1091 Q: On what side of Memorial Stadium is the Big Red "N" located?

1092 Q: What number did Bill Thornton wear for the Huskers?

1093 Q: What college football team plays in the same stadium as the Orange Bowl?

1094 Q: What was the point spread in the 1993 Orange Bowl?

1095 Q: Who in the 1920-30's proclaimed the University of Nebraska Band "the finest in America"?

1096 Q: What amount of money was budgeted in 1880 for the university band in it's first year?

1097 Q: What was the first Nebraska University band called?

1098 Q: In what city is Big Twelve opponent Baylor located?

1099 Q: Name one of the two minor league baseball organizations for which Turner Gill played.

1100 Q: Turner Gill suffered a leg injury that almost ended his football career. In which game did that occur?

1085 A: He vomited from exhaustion.

1086 A: Calvin Jones

1087 A: Austin, TX

1088 A: College Station, TX

1089 A: Lubbock, Texas

1090 A: Georgia

1091 A: The west side

1092 A: 30

1093 A: Miami Hurricanes

1094 A: Florida State to beat NU by 17

1095 A: John Philip Sousa

1096 A: $150.00

1097 A: The University of Nebraska Military Cadet Band

1098 A: Waco, Texas

1099 A: Cleveland and Detroit

1100 A: The 1981 Iowa State game

1101 Q: What is the home town of Husker great Jerry Tagge?

1102 Q: What is the name of Big Eight rival Oklahoma's field?

1103 Q: What was the name of the arena in which the Husker men's basketball team first played?

1104 Q: Which Nebraska tight end later became a state senator?

1105 Q: Who does Nebraska face in the 1995 football opener?

1106 Q: Out of the last 14 seasons, how many times have the Huskers played the eventual national champion in football?

1107 Q: Which Big Eight school did the Husker football team encounter first in the 1995 season?

1108 Q: What is the actual name of the cheerleaders for the Huskers?

1109 Q: Which member of the 1971 championship football team was killed in an airplane crash in the 1990's?

1110 Q: Who at Nebraska was nicknamed "The Senator" in the 1940's?

1111 Q: Which Husker from the 1950's was known as the "Cambridge Crusher"?

1112 Q: What does State Senator Ernie Chambers legislative bill propose for NU football players?

1113 Q: How many meters around is Nebraska's outdoor track?

1114 Q: What was the name of the NU school newspaper that covered Husker athletics in the 1920's?

1115 Q: Within 100 students, what was the university enrollment in Nebraska's first year in the Missouri Valley conference?

1101 A: Green Bay, WI

1102 A: Owen Field

1103 A: Grant Hall

1104 A: Jim McFarland

1105 A: Oklahoma State

1106 A: 10

1107 A: Oklahoma State

1108 A: The Yell Squad

1109 A: Jerry List

1110 A: Ray "The Senator" Prochaska

1111 A: Jerry Minnick

1112 A. To pay them as state employees

1113 A: 400 meters

1114 A: The Hesperian

1115 A: 3,237

1116 Q: What is the name of the Husker baseball clubhouse?

1117 Q: How many feet on the foul line is home plate to the fence in Buck Beltzer Stadium?

1118 Q: What radio station broadcasts NU baseball games?

1119 Q: What is the headline on the front of the January 9, 1995 issue of Sports Illustrated?

1120 Q: What Lincoln area business carried the original "Big Red Collection" retail goods?

1121 Q: How many feet straight away to center field is the fence at Buck Beltzer Stadium?

1122 Q: What sports magazine covering Husker athletics is published in Nebraska?

1123 Q: What Husker athletic director is famous for his speeches in the men's locker room prior to NCAA gymnastics championships?

1124 Q: What is the name of the trivia game created to educate and entertain consumers about NU athletics?

1125 Q: How many sprint lanes are there on the Ed Weir track?

1126 Q: Who is the Chief of Staff for the Department of Athletic Medicine at Nebraska?

1127 Q: What retail store in Lincoln sells the largest quantity of Husker goods?

1128 Q: Who is the Head Athletic Trainer for the University?

1129 Q: Where is the Nebraska athletic ticket office located?

1130 Q: What percent discount do NU students receive on season tickets for football and basketball?

1116 A: The Baumann Building

1117 A: 330 feet

1118 A: KLIN

1119 A: "How Sweet It Is!"

1120 A: The Nebraska Bookstore

1121 A: 400 feet

1122 A: Nebraska Sports Magazine

1123 A: Bob Devaney

1124 A: Husker Sports Trivia

1125 A: Eight

1126 A: Dr. Pat Clare

1127 A: The Nebraska Bookstore

1128 A: Jerry Weber

1129 A: In the South Stadium office building

1130 A: 50 percent discount

1131 Q: What is the name of Nebraska's athletic ticket office manager?

1132 Q: What three sports offer reserved seating for home contests at NU?

1133 Q: In how many different locations is the NU athletic department housed?

1134 Q: What is the name of the NU women's gymnastics team training facility?

1135 Q: On what street is Memorial Stadium located?

1136 Q: What is the "N" club?

1137 Q: In which direction is the 100 meter sprint run at Ed Weir track?

1138 Q: What is the name of the distinguished group of major donors to the University of Nebraska?

1139 Q: How many Outland Trophy winners has NU football produced through 1995?

1140 Q: How many NU receivers have caught 4 touchdown passes in a single game?

1141 Q: Who was the sole All-American performer for the NU wrestling team in 1994?

1142 Q: In which season did the Huskers lead the nation in scoring defense?

1143 Q: Which Husker had the most interceptions for touchdowns in a single season?

1144 Q: Which Husker had the most unassisted tackles in his career?

1145 Q: In what year did the Huskers post their highest batting average?

1131 A: Cindy Bell

1132 A: Football, men's basketball and volleyball

1133 A: Seven

1134 A: Mabel Lee Hall

1135 A: Stadium Drive

1136 A: An organization of former Husker letter-winners

1137 A: East

1138 A: The Chancellor's Club

1139 A: Seven

1140 A: None

1141 A: Scott Gonyo

1142 A: In 1984 Nebraska led with 9.5 points per game.

1143 A: Dave Mason picked off three to score in 1971.

1144 A: Steve Damkroger had 157.

1145 A: In 1985 Nebraska hit .339

1146 Q: What was NU's longest bowl game run for a touch-down?

1147 Q: How many victories did Gale Sayers lead the Kansas Jayhawks to against the Husk ers?

1148 Q: Who was the greatest quarterback in NU history in terms of passing percentage?

1146 A: Dennis Claridge in the 1964 Orange Bowl ran for a 68 yard TD.

1147 A: None

1148 A: Jerry Tagge completed 348 out of 581 passes between 1969-71 for a .598 completion percentage.

1113 Q: How many meters around is Nebraska's out-door track?

4. History

1237 Q: When was NU's fight song, "There is no Place Like Nebraska" adopted?

1149 Q: When was the first "Band Day" held in Memorial Stadium?

1150 Q: In what year did the Nebraska marching band begin playing at football games?

1151 Q: What is the name of the sportscaster who was the voice of Husker football on KFAB radio?

1152 Q: When was the Husker football team first broadcast on national television?

1153 Q: What Missouri Valley team did the Huskers face in their first NCAA playoff game in men's basketball?

1154 Q: When did Nebraska install artificial turf in Memorial Stadium?

1155 Q: When was the first televised game at Memorial Stadium?

1156 Q: In what year did Nebraska add a single red stripe to the all-white helmets?

1157 Q: In what year did the Bob Devaney Sports Center open?

1158 Q: In what year did NU play its first football game in Memorial Stadium?

1159 Q: In what year did NU football have its first undefeated season?

1160 Q: What team did NU defeat in the 1971 Orange Bowl?

1161 Q: When was the last time an NU men's basketball player scored over 40 points in a single game?

1162 Q: What team did the 1994 National Champion Huskers defeat in the Kickoff Classic at East Rutherford, N.J.?

1163 Q: When were the Huskers last shut out in Memorial Stadium?

1149 A: 10 high school bands were first invited to play in 1939.

1150 A: 1890

1151 A: Lyle Bremser

1152 A: In 1953 against Oregon

1153 A: Oklahoma A&M

1154 A: 1970

1155 A: 1953 against Oregon

1156 A: 1967

1157 A: 1976

1158 A: 1923

1159 A: 1890

1160 A: Louisiana State University

1161 A: 1994, Eric Piatkowski

1162 A: West Virginia

1163 A: Kansas State shut out NU in 1968.

1164 Q: Which Husker led the Big Eight in scoring in 1964?

1165 Q: Combining the 1959 and 1960 seasons, how many touchdown passes did the NU football team throw: 1, 4, 8 or 12?

1166 Q: What football team did NU defeat in its first football game in 1890?

1167 Q: In what year did the Husker baseball team win 26 consecutive games to set an all-time Nebraska school record?

1168 Q: In what year did the NU football team allow the least amount of total yardage per game?

1169 Q: Which NU football player led the Big Eight in scoring in 1970?

1170 Q: In what year did the Husker football team average over 400 yards rushing per game?

1171 Q: In what year did Tom Osborne's Huskers shut out three teams consecutively?

1172 Q: What did Husker athlete Scott Hooper steal in 1984?

1173 Q: Who was football's Big Eight Player-of-the-Year in 1970?

1174 Q: Name two of the four captains of the 1983 Nebraska football team.

1175 Q: Who was selected by the Baltimore Colts in the first round of the1974 NFL draft?

1176 Q: Which Nebraska football player is the only member of the Pro Football Hall of Fame and the National Football Foundation Hall of Fame?

1177 Q: With the great Scott Hooper leading the way how many stolen bases did the Husk ers pilfer in 1984: 122, 146, 175 or 196?

1164 A: Kent McCloughan led the way with 74 points.

1165 A: one

1166 A: Omaha YMCA

1167 A: 1983

1168 A: 1940

1169 A: Joe Orduna led all scorers with 92 points.

1170 A: 1983

1171 A: In 1979 the Huskers shut out New Mexico State, Kansas and Oklahoma State.

1172 A: 60 bases for NU's baseball team

1173 A: Jerry Murtaugh

1174 A: Turner Gill, Mike Keeler, Dean Steinkuhler and Mike Tranmer

1175 A: Nebraska's John Dutton

1176 A: Guy Chamberlain

1177 A: 196

1178 Q: Who were the Nebraska first round draft choices in the 1979 NFL draft?

1179 Q: Which NFL team chose Junior Miller in the first round of the 1980 NFL draft?

1180 Q: In the year that Mike Rozier won the Heisman Trophy, what Husker teammate finished fourth in the balloting?

1181 Q: How many times has the NU volleyball team been runner-up to a national championship?

1182 Q: Which Nebraska defensive end was chosen in the first round of the NFL draft in 1988?

1183 Q: Who were the first Nebraska football players to participate in the Senior Bowl?

1184 Q: Name the first three athletes inducted into the Nebraska football Hall of Fame.

1185 Q: Who was Nebraska's first African-American "All-American"?

1186 Q: In what year did the NU volleyball team hold the #1 position on the polls longer than any other school?

1187 Q: What was the result of Nebraska's first Orange Bowl contest against the Crimson Tide of Alabama?

1188 Q: What was the final play of the 1994 Orange Bowl?

1189 Q: In NU's last ten bowl games (including the 1995 Orange Bowl), how many of their opponents were ranked higher than the Huskers?

1190 Q: How many times in the 1980's did the NU volleyball team make the NCAA tournament?

1191 Q: How many pass interceptions did NU record against Georgia in the 1969 Sun Bowl to set a Husker record?

1178 A: George Andrews and Kelvin Clark

1179 A: Atlanta Falcons

1180 A: Turner Gill

1181 A: Two times: 1986 and 1989

1182 A: Neil Smith

1183 A: Joe Bordogna and Jerry Minnick in 1953

1184 A: Ed Weir, Guy Chamberlain and George Sauer

1185 A: Bob Brown in 1963

1186 A: 1994

1187 A: They were defeated 39-28 in 1965.

1188 A: NU's Byron Bennett missed a 45 yard field goal.

1189 A: 8 out of the 10 were ranked higher.

1190 A: Eight; 1982-1989

1191 A: Six

1192 Q: What team did the Huskers go up against in the 1977 Liberty Bowl?

1193 Q: After leading the nation in turnover margin with a +18 in 1992, how many turnovers did the Huskers commit in the Orange Bowl following that great season?

1194 Q: NU played in the first ever "night" bowl game. When was this?

1195 Q: Which two Huskers switched jerseys in the 1984 Orange Bowl to confuse the Miami offense?

1196 Q: Until the 1993-94 academic year, how many consecutive Big Eight Conference all-sport championships had the Huskers won?

1197 Q: When was the last time that a Kansas football team defeated Nebraska?

1198 Q: What lightweight opponent shut out the Husker football team in the 1955 season opener?

1199 Q: What conference did the Huskers swimmers rule during the 1930's?

1200 Q: Name the two Division 1-AA football opponents that NU faced in the 1990's.

1201 Q: Prior to Penn State joining the Big Ten conference, Tom Osborne's Huskers lost to three opponents from that league. Name them.

1202 Q: What conference did Nebraska help form in 1928?

1203 Q: When was Shulte Field House completed?

1204 Q: When was the last time an NU football team has not been ranked in an AP poll?

1205 Q: In which season did the Nebraska football team play its 1000th game?

1192 A: North Carolina

1193 A: An unbelievable seven

1194 A: In 1966 the Huskers played Alabama in the Orange Bowl.

1195 A: Dave Burke and Mike McCashland

1196 A: 15

1197 A: In 1968, when Kansas also tied for the Big Eight title.

1198 A: Hawaii beat NU 6-0.

1199 A: The Big Six

1200 A: Middle Tennessee State and North Texas State

1201 A: Wisconsin in 1974, Iowa in 1981 and Michigan in 1986

1202 A: The Big Six

1203 A: In 1946

1204 A: NU has been included in every poll since 1981.

1205 A: In 1993 when NU defeated Kansas

1206 Q: How many times in the 1990's has the Nebraska football team faced the team that ended the season #1 in the polls?

1207 Q: In 1990 NU lost to the two teams that eventually tied for the national championship. Who were those teams?

1208 Q: When was artificial turf first installed in Memorial Stadium?

1209 Q: In what year was NU's first night home football game?

1210 Q: Who were the co-captains of the 1971 Nebraska football team?

1211 Q: How many times has the NU football team played 12 games in the regular season?

1212 Q: Who were the two teams that the NU football team beat by only one point in the 1993 season?

1213 Q: Who were the three NU football players that won Super Bowl rings with the San Francisco 49ers after the 1989 season?

1214 Q: What anniversary did the University of Nebraska celebrate in 1994?

1215 Q: What was the reason Biff Jones left the football team at NU in 1941?

1216 Q: How many points did the NU football team score in the second half of the 1983 game against Colorado to set a Big Eight record?

1217 Q: Which team led the Big Eight conference in touchdown passes during the 1980 season?

1218 Q: In what year was the NU men's basketball team a No. 3 seed in the region in the NCAA tournament?

1219 Q: How many rushing yards did NU gain against New Mexico State in 1982 to break a school record: 524, 588, 621 or 677?

1206 A: Five: Colorado, Georgia Tech, Washington, Miami and Florida State

1207 A: Colorado and Georgia Tech

1208 A: 1970

1209 A: They met Florida State under the lights in 1986.

1210 A: Jerry Tagge and Jim Anderson

1211 A: Six times including the 1994 championship season

1212 A: UCLA and Kansas

1213 A: Roger Craig, Tom Rathman and Jamie Williams

1214 A: 125th anniversary

1215 A: He was recalled into active service with the Army.

1216 A: 55

1217 A: Nebraska

1218 A: 1991

1219 A: An unbelievable 677

1220 Q: How many times have the Huskers traveled to El Paso, Texas to play in the Sun Bowl?

1221 Q: How many consecutive years has Nebraska played on New Year's Day, including the 1995 Orange Bowl?

1222 Q: When was Buck Beltzer Stadium dedicated?

1223 Q: What was the final year "Mr. Husker" Lyle Bremser worked NU football games for KFAB radio?

1224 Q: How many years did Lyle Bremser broadcast NU football games before his retirement?

1225 Q: What team ended the Husker's most-successful season by knocking them out of the first round of the NCAA basketball tournament in 1991?

1226 Q: When did Nebraska football begin recruiting junior college athletes from the West Coast?

1227 Q: Who was the famous headliner for the "Double Hundred Celebration" banquet?

1228 Q: Who was NU's last opponent at Nebraska Field?

1229 Q: Before the loss to NU in 1959, how many years had the Sooners of Oklahoma gone undefeated in the Big Eight?

1230 Q: How many undefeated seasons has the men's basketball team at Nebraska had?

1231 Q: Who beat the NU football team 13-12 in 1973 after Nebraska's two-point conversion attempt was intercepted?

1232 Q: Husker great George Flippin led NU to its first victory over an out-of-state rival. Who was the opponent?

1233 Q: In what year were the official team colors adopted at Nebraska?

1234 Q: Who was the first Husker football player selected to the Walter Camp All-American team?

1220 A: Two times: 1969 and 1980

1221 A: 14 years straight

1222 A: 1980

1223 A: 1983

1224 A: 45 years

1225 A: Xavier

1226 A: Following back-to-back 6-4 seasons in 1967 and 1968

1227 A: Bob Hope

1228 A: Notre Dame

1229 A: An unbelievable thirteen years

1230 A: Three: 1896-97, 1898-99 and 1899-1900

1231 A: Missouri

1232 A: Iowa

1233 A: 1892

1234 A: Vic Halligan in 1914

1235 Q: How many seasons has the NU men's basketball team had without a single win?

1236 Q: Name the Husker who gained 126 yards on 17 carries, leading NU to defeat Florida in the 1974 Sugar Bowl.

1237 Q: When was NU's fight song, "There is no Place Like Nebraska" adopted?

1238 Q: How many games had the Huskers played in Buck Beltzer Stadium before hitting a home run?

1239 Q: Who wrote NU's fight song "There is no Place Like Nebraska"?

1240 Q: In what year was the University of Nebraska founded?

1241 Q: What season did the NU men's basketball team capture the first Missouri Valley conference title?

1242 Q: How many No. 1 teams in school history has the NU men's basketball team knocked off?

1243 Q: How many times in the 1980's did the NU men's gymnastics team win a Big Eight championship?

1244 Q: How many individual Big Eight titles did gymnast Scott Johnson win in 1983?

1245 Q: Who was the last Husker football player to serve as a team captain two years in a row?

1246 Q: Name NU's first participant in the Shrine Bowl game.

1247 Q: Knute Rockne said this NU back "beat us out of two championships" in 1922 and 1923. Name this Husker.

1248 Q: Teammates Anthony Steels and Walter Wallace played prep football in which foreign countries?

1249 Q: Against which Big Ten school did the NU men's basketball team first compete?

1235 A: Zero (NU's least amount of wins was 1 in 1897-98)

1236 A: Tony Davis

1237 A: 1923

1238 A: Just one game

1239 A: Henry Pecha

1240 A: 1869

1241 A: 1911-12

1242 A: Three: Kansas in 1958, Michigan in 1964-65 and Missouri in 1981-82

1243 A: Seven

1244 A: Five

1245 A: Robert Mullen in 1950-51

1246 A: Harold Hutchinson

1247 A: Dave Noble

1248 A: Spain and Italy, respectively

1249 A: Wisconsin

1250 Q: Name the famous NU fullback that placed fourth in the shot put during the 1936 Olympic Games.

1251 Q: When was the press box added to Memorial Stadium?

1252 Q: When was the lighting system dedicated at Buck Beltzer Stadium?

1253 Q: When was the first additional seating added to Memorial Stadium?

1254 Q: When did the Memorial Stadium sellout streak start?

1255 Q: When was the first night game played at Memorial Stadium?

1256 Q: What player in 1970 became the first Husker men's basketball player to average 20 or more points per game?

1257 Q: When was the top season for Nebraska football home game attendance?

1258 Q: How many times did OU lead in the 1971 Nebraska/Oklahoma game?

1259 Q: How many times did the Blackshirts sack Penn State quarterbacks in the 21-7 victory of 1980: three, six nine or twelve?

1260 Q: What was the worst decade in school history for the men's gymnastics program?

1261 Q: Name one of the two defensive ends from the 1980 Husker football team who supplied NU with so many spectacular efforts.

1262 Q: Which OU back scored the winning touchdown in the 1980 Nebraska/Oklahoma game?

1263 Q: When was the first time in school history for the men's basketball team to record back-to-back 20-win seasons?

1250 A: Sam Francis

1251 A: 1964

1252 A: 1990

1253 A: 1964

1254 A: 1962

1255 A: 1986

1256 A: Marvin Stewart

1257 A: 1983

1258 A: Two times: Halftime and fourth quarter

1259 A: Nine

1260 A: The 1970's

1261 A: Derrie Nelson or Jimmie Williams

1262 A: George "Buster" Rhymes

1263 A: 1993-94 seasons

1264 Q: Name the Husker who intercepted a last-minute Oklahoma pass and preserved an NU victory in 1982.

1265 Q: Name the fullback that scored two touchdowns in the 1982 Nebraska victory over Oklahoma.

1266 Q: After losing to Nebraska 63-7 in 1983, this East Coast team shocked the Huskers football team by winning 17-9 the following season.

1267 Q: Whose field goal with six seconds left in the game gave Oklahoma a victory over Nebraska in 1986?

1268 Q: Which team did NU defeat in the first and only Big Eight Holiday Basketball Tournament in 1967?

1269 Q: How many players took the field for the Huskers in Nebraska's first game of 1890?

1270 Q: Name the halfback who played from 1892-94 who was arguably Nebraska's first football star.

1271 Q: How many Big Eight championships did the men's gymnastics team win in the 1980's?

1272 Q: Who won the game in the first football meeting between Nebraska and Kansas?

1273 Q: Name the player who scored 16 points by kicking four field goals and four extra points in the 1969 Sun Bowl.

1274 Q: Name the first NU athlete to compete in the Olympic Games.

1275 Q: Which female Husker athlete was the Honda/Broderick award winner for the sport of volleyball in the 1986-87 season?

1276 Q: Who was favored to win the Nebraska/USC game in the 1970 championship season?

1264 A: Scott Strasburger

1265 A: Doug Wilkening

1266 A: Syracuse

1267 A: Tim Lashar

1268 A: Kansas State

1269 A: At that time 9 players at a time were allowed on the field.

1270 A: George Flippin

1271 A: Seven

1272 A: Kansas won 12-0 in 1892.

1273 A: Paul Rogers

1274 A: Lewis Anderson ran the 1500 meters in 1912.

1275 A: Karen Dahlgren

1276 A: Southern California by 14

1277 Q: Name the first Nebraska football player to incline press 300 pounds.

1278 Q: Name the defensive tackle from Nebraska who was named outstanding lineman of the year in 1971.

1279 Q: Name the All-American tackle from the 1971 championship team who had an arm span of 7 feet.

1280 Q: Who defeated Nebraska in the National Championships of Men's Gymnastics in 1995?

1281 Q: Who is the 1981 All-American defensive end that walked on to the Husker team at 180 pounds?

1282 Q: Who was named the MVP of the 1980 Japan Bowl?

1283 Q: How many concerts did the Husker athletic department host in 1993-94?

1284 Q: During what two years after joining the Missouri Valley Conference did the Nebraska football team play as an independent?

1285 Q: Which Big Eight team was the last to join in 1957?

1286 Q: In what year did the Big Eight fully involve women into athletics with financial and administrative support?

1287 Q: What team did Nebraska defeat in the 1974 Sugar Bowl?

1288 Q: Which Husker football player in 1993 was named "NU's little big man"?

1289 Q: In what years did the NU football team win national championships?

1290 Q: Which reserve quarterback helped NU mount a fourth quarter comeback to win the 1974 Sugar Bowl?

1277 A: Bob Newton

1278 A: Larry Jacobson

1279 A: John Dutton

1280 A: Stanford

1281 A: Jimmie Williams

1282 A: I.M. Hipp

1283 A: 12

1284 A: 1919-20

1285 A: Oklahoma

1286 A: 1979

1287 A: Florida

1288 A: Barron Miles

1289 A: 1970, 1971 and 1994

1290 A: Terry Luck

1291 Q: Who did NU lose to in the 1965 Cotton Bowl?

1292 Q: Which NU player provided the winning score in the 1974 Sugar Bowl?

1293 Q: Name the kicker from Arizona State who booted the winning field goal in the 1975 Fiesta Bowl.

1294 Q: What ended the Huskers' comeback hopes in the 1975 Fiesta Bowl?

1295 Q: Name the Clemson kicker who connected on 3 field goals and helped Clemson sink the Huskers in the 1982 Orange bowl.

1296 Q: Who did Nebraska defeat in the 1980 Sun Bowl?

1297 Q: Name the Husker who scored the first touchdown in the 1941 Rose Bowl.

1298 Q: Name the player who came off the bench for Nebraska and threw two touchdown passes in the 1977 Liberty Bowl.

1299 Q: Which Husker caught the winning touchdown pass in the 1977 Liberty Bowl?

1300 Q: Who was named the most valuable defensive player in the 1977 Liberty Bowl?

1301 Q: What teams were upset in January, 1971 to lead the way for Nebraska's national championship?

1302 Q: To which team did Nebraska lose in the 1986 Fiesta Bowl?

1303 Q: What trick play set up a Husker touchdown in the 1980 Cotton bowl and gave NU a 14-10 lead?

1304 Q: What year was the first for the Husker football team to lift weights during the season?

1291 A: Arkansas

1292 A: Kicker Mike Coyle

1293 A: Dan Kush

1294 A: A Tony Davis' fumble

1295 A: Donald Igwebuike

1296 A: Mississippi State

1297 A: Vike Francis

1298 A: Randy Garcia

1299 A: Tim Smith

1300 A: George Andrews

1301 A: No. 1 Texas and No. 2 Ohio State

1302 A: Michigan

1303 A: A Jarvis Redwine's pass to Jeff Quinn

1304 A: 1970

1305 Q: In 1974 who was the first Husker to bench press 400 pounds?

1306 Q: In 1986 who was the first Husker to bench press 500 pounds?

1307 Q: When did the football team add stripes to the sleeves of their uniforms?

1308 Q: Which team defeated Nebraska in the 1989 Orange Bowl?

1309 Q: When was "There is no Place Like Nebraska," written?

1310 Q: Whose all-white attire made him stand out among Husker football fans in the 1970's and 80's?

1311 Q: Who did NU play in the post-season charity game of 1918?

1312 Q: Which team played the Huskers in the first game in Memorial Stadium?

1313 Q: Which team defeated Nebraska in the 1990 Fiesta Bowl?

1314 Q: In what year was the Husker football team first ranked in the AP poll?

1315 Q: In what year did the Memorial Stadium seating capacity go from 31,080 to 44,829?

1316 Q: In what year did the Memorial Stadium seating capacity go from 44,829 to 50,807?

1317 Q: In what year did the Memorial Stadium seating capacity go from 50,807 to 62,644?

1318 Q: In what year did the Memorial Stadium seating capacity go from 62,644 to 64,170?

1305 A: Lawrence Cooley

1306 A: Lawrence Pete

1307 A: 1969

1308 A: Miami

1309 A: 1923

1310 A: Husker Bob

1311 A: Washington University of St. Louis, MO

1312 A: Oklahoma

1313 A: Florida State

1314 A: 1936

1315 A: 1964

1316 A: 1965

1317 A: 1966

1318 A: 1967

1319 Q: Who defeated Nebraska in the 1982 Orange Bowl?

1320 Q: In what year did the seating capacity in memorial Stadium increase to 73,650?

1321 Q: Who did Nebraska defeat in the 1964 Orange Bowl?

1322 Q: Who beat Nebraska in the 1967 Sugar Bowl?

1323 Q: Name the first band to visit Nebraska in 1900 to support their athletic team.

1324 Q: What Big Twelve expansion team did NU defeat in the 1974 Cotton Bowl?

1325 Q: How many undefeated "regular seasons" has Tom Osborne had?

1326 Q: Which team was responsible for Tom Osborne's first bowl game loss?

1327 Q: Which team stopped the Husker football team from an undefeated season in 1982?

1328 Q: In what year did NU first field a men's basketball team?

1329 Q: What bowl game did Nebraska play indoors in 1976?

1330 Q: Which team did Nebraska defeat in the 1977 Liberty Bowl?

1331 Q: To which team did NU lose in the 1980 Cotton Bowl?

1332 Q: Who was the first opponent for the Husker men's basketball team?

1333 Q: Which team defeated NU in the 1988 Fiesta Bowl?

1334 Q: How many members were there in the first NU band in 1880?

1319 A: Clemson

1320 A: 1972

1321 A: Auburn

1322 A: Alabama

1323 A: Minnesota

1324 A: Texas

1325 A: Three

1326 A: Arizona State

1327 A: Penn State

1328 A: 1897

1329 A: The 1976 Astro-Bluebonnet Bowl

1330 A: North Carolina

1331 A: Houston

1332 A: The Lincoln YMCA

1333 A: Florida State

1334 A: Twelve

1335 Q: At what sporting event did the NU band first perform?

1336 Q: The 1898 NU football season ended in a financial deficit. What event was staged to recover some of the loss?

1337 Q: When did the men's basketball team at NU play other university teams for the first time?

1338 Q: In 1978, what did Rick Berns do on the field after the OU game?

1339 Q: How many times in the 1980-90's has NU failed to produce a 1000 yard rusher?

1340 Q: In what game in 1979 was Jarvis Redwine injured on a PAT?

1341 Q: In the 1950 Husker football season, how many times did the great Bobby Reynolds score all of NU's points?

1342 Q: When did the NU men's basketball team first play teams from outside Nebraska?

1343 Q: Which NU back filled in for Joe Orduna when he went down with a knee injury in 1969?

1344 Q: Why did the Huskers appear in the 1954 Orange Bowl in spite of losing to Oklahoma?

1345 Q: Where were the Huskers placed to finish in the Big Eight for the 1994-95 basketball season after winning the post-season tournament the previous year?

1346 Q: How many consecutive winning seasons did the Nebraska football team have going into the 1995 season?

1347 Q: Who was the NU men's basketball first out-of-state opponent?

1348 Q: Through the 1994 season, in how many consecutive bowl games have the Huskers appeared?

1335 A: A baseball game against Kansas State in 1887

1336 A: The "Football Vaudeville" show

1337 A: 1899

1338 A: A back flip

1339 A: Only two times: 1986 and 1990

1340 A: The Missouri game

1341 A: Three times

1342 A: 1900

1343 A: Jeff Kinney

1344 A: There was a no-repeat rule in the Big Eight.

1345 A: Fourth

1346 A: 33

1347 A: Kansas

1348 A: 26

1349 Q: Who was the All-American end on the 1971 championship football team?

1350 Q: What was unique about Husker star Bob Mehring's football shoes in the 1930's?

1351 Q: Who was the conference scoring leader on the 1936 Husker football team?

1352 Q: Which two present-day Big Eight men's basketball teams were the first to play one another?

1353 Q: In what year did the Nebraska football team first use the "Bounceroosky" trick play?

1354 Q: Which Husker did Pop Warner call, "the greatest tackle who ever lived"?

1355 Q: Which Husker made the final block to spring Johnny Rodgers free on his famous punt return against OU?

1356 Q: Name one of the three Huskers selected in the first round of the 1937 NFL draft.

1357 Q: What present-day Big Ten team was the only team to defeat the men's basketball team at NU in 1911?

1358 Q: Name one of the two All-American ends in 1965 for the Huskers.

1359 Q: Which Husker was named Big Eight defensive player of the year in 1993?

1360 Q: Who was the first All-Big Eight football player for the Huskers?

1361 Q: On what did the NU men's basketball team blame their only loss in 1911?

1362 Q: Which player from Nebraska was named All-Pro in his rookie year of the 1993 NFL season?

1349 A: Willie Harper

1350 A: He made them himself.

1351 A: Lloyd Cardwell

1352 A: Kansas and Nebraska

1353 A: Against OU in 1982

1354 A: Ed Weir

1355 A: Joe Blahak

1356 A: Lloyd Cardwell, Sam Francis and Les McDonald

1357 A: Minnesota

1358 A: Tony Jetter and Freeman White

1359 A: Trev Alberts

1360 A: Don Olson in 1959

1361 A: The Minnesota Gophers had a 100-foot floor.

1362 A: Tyrone Hughes with the New Orleans Saints

1363 Q: Who was Nebraska's first player from the 1920's in the Shrine East-West game?

1364 Q: What was the last game Nebraska lost before winning the national championship in 1970?

1365 Q: What two Missouri Valley teams shared the conference basketball title in 1912 and 1914?

1366 Q: Why did the Huskers not go to the Orange Bowl after they tied for the Big Eight title in 1969?

1367 Q: What did Don Bryant do prior to coming to NU as the sports information director?

1368 Q: Which Big Eight football opponent is the third longest athletic series in Nebraska history?

1369 Q: In what year did Nebraska win its first Missouri Valley basketball title outright?

1370 Q: How were the improvements for Buck Beltzer Stadium financed in 1977?

1371 Q: How many All-American male swimmers did the Huskers have in 1988?

1372 Q: How much did KFAB initially pay for the right to exclusively broadcast NU football and basketball games?

1373 Q: Within 5 million, how many television viewers were tuned to the 1971 game of the century?

1374 Q: What was the score of the 1941 Rose Bowl?

1375 Q: Which present-day Big Eight team defeated the Husker men's basketball team in their first game in the Coliseum?

1376 Q: When was the last time Nebraska gave up a kickoff return for a touchdown?

1363 A: Harold Hutchison

1364 A: NU lost to Missouri in 1969.

1365 A: Nebraska and Kansas

1366 A: Missouri beat NU during the season and claimed a share of the title.

1367 A: He was the Sports Editor for the Lincoln Star.

1368 A: Missouri

1369 A: 1916

1370 A: Contributions from the Californians for Nebraska boosters

1371 A: 11

1372 A: $2.5 million

1373 A: 55 million

1374 A: Nebraska-13, Stanford-21

1375 A: Kansas

1254 Q: When did the Memorial Stadium sellout streak start?

5. Records

1479 Q: Who owns the Husker men's gymnastics record on the pommel horse?

1377 Q: Against what non-conference football team has NU lost the most games?

1378 Q: What NU receiver had the highest average gain per pass reception in his career?

1379 Q: When was the first time the men's basketball team at Nebraska played in the National Invitation Tournament?

1380 Q: Who had the longest run from scrimmage in the 1995 Orange Bowl?

1381 Q: How many consecutive bowl games had NU lost prior to the 1995 Orange Bowl?

1382 Q: Which Husker quarterback had the most rushing attempts in his career?

1383 Q: Which quarterback holds an NU record for passing percentage in a single game?

1384 Q: Which Husker quarterback carried the ball the most during a single season?

1385 Q: In what year did the men's basketball team record its first 20 win season?

1386 Q: Which Husker quarterback threw the longest touchdown pass in NU history?

1387 Q: Which NU quarterback holds the record for the most interceptions?

1388 Q: Which NU quarterback holds the record for the most consecutive pass attempts without an interception?

1389 Q: Which Husker quarterback holds the school record for most pass completions in a single season?

1390 Q: Which Husker quarterback holds the school record for most passing yards in a single season?

1377 A: University of Pittsburgh with a record of (4-15-3)

1378 A: Rob Schnitzler

1379 A: 1967

1380 A: Lawrence Phillips and Tommie Frazier both had gains of 25 yards.

1381 A: Seven

1382 A: Steve Taylor had 431 carries for 2125 yards between 1985-88.

1383 A: Turner Gill was 11 of 12 in 1982 versus Kansas State.

1384 A: Steve Taylor carried the ball 157 times in 1988.

1385 A: 1965-66 season

1386 A: Fred Duda had a 95 yard TD pass against Colorado in 1965.

1387 A: Dave Humm was picked off 36 times.

1388 A: Turner Gill with 125

1389 A: Vince Ferragamo completed 145 passes in 1976.

1390 A: Dave Humm passed for 2074 yards in 1972.

1391 Q: What Husker won the Naismith Award in 1982?

1392 Q: Which Husker quarterback gained the most yards rushing in a single game?

1393 Q: Which Husker quarterback holds the NU record for passing yardage in a single game?

1394 Q: Which Nebraska quarterback gained the most rushing yards in a single season?

1395 Q: Who was the first three-time academic All-Big Eight pick in Nebraska basketball history?

1396 Q: Which NU quarterback scored four touchdowns in the 1985 Sugar Bowl victory?

1397 Q: Which NU fullback rushed for a school record nine touchdowns in a single season?

1398 Q: Name the Nebraska players who had the longest touchdown run in school history.

1399 Q: Which Husker quarterback has thrown the most touchdown passes in a single game?

1400 Q: Who was Nebraska's leading rusher in 1976?

1401 Q: Which NU fullback owns the record for rushing attempts in a single game?

1402 Q: Which Husker holds the men's school basketball record for free-throw percentage?

1403 Q: What NU running back had the longest touchdown run from scrimmage in 1983?

1404 Q: Which Husker fullback gained the most rushing yards in his collegiate career?

1405 Q: In 1988 NU's Bobby Benjamin set a school record by hitting how many home runs in a season?

1391 A: Jack Moore

1392 A: Gerry Gdowski ran for 174 yards against Iowa State in 1989.

1393 A: Dave Humm had 297 yards against Wisconsin in 1973.

1394 A: Gerry Gdowski ran for 925 yards in 1989.

1395 A: Jack Moore

1396 A: Craig Sundberg

1397 A: Mark Schellen rushed for nine TD's in 1983.

1398 A: Craig Johnson in 1979 and Roger Craig in 1981 each had 94 yard runs for scores.

1399 A: Steve Taylor had five TD throws against UCLA in 1987.

1400 A: Rick Burns with 854 yards

1401 A: Jerry Brown had 25 carries in 1956 against Baylor.

1402 A: Jack Moore

1403 A: Paul Miles scored on a 78 yard run against Kansas.

1404 A: Andra Franklin ran for 1738 yards between 1977-80.

1405 A: 21

1406 Q: Which Husker had the longest run that did not result in a touchdown?

1407 Q: Which football player had the most all-purpose running yards in a season for Nebraska?

1408 Q: What NCAA record did Husker great Bobby Reynolds hold for 38 years?

1409 Q: Who were the first pair of Husker rushers to each gain over 100 yards in the same game?

1410 Q: How many runs did Ken Ramos score in 1988 to set a new school baseball record?

1411 Q: When was the last time a Husker running back rushed for less than 1000 yards yet still led Nebraska in total rushing yardage?

1412 Q: Which Nebraska player had the most pass receptions in a single game?

1413 Q: In what year did the NU men's basketball team earn its first "official" berth into the NCAA tournament?

1414 Q: Which Nebraska receiver had the highest average gain per pass reception in his career: Johnny Rodgers, Rob Schnitzler or Irving Fryar?

1415 Q: Which Husker had the most yards in pass receptions in a single game?

1416 Q: What Nebraska pitcher had 123 strikeouts in 1993 to set a school record?

1417 Q: What Husker back had the most all-purpose running yards in a single game?

1418 Q: Within five yards, what was Calvin Jones' longest run from scrimmage to score a touchdown?

1406 A: I.M. Hipp had a 74 yard run in 1977 that did not produce a score.

1407 A: Mike Rozier earned this record in 1983 with 2486 yards.

1408 A: A scoring record of 17.4 points per game

1409 A: Tony Davis and John O'Leary against Kansas State in 1973

1410 A: 100

1411 A: In 1990 Leodis Flowers led NU in rushing with 940 yards.

1412 A: Dennis Richnafsky had 14 receptions against Kansas State in 1967.

1413 A: 1986

1414 A: Rob Schnitzler averaged 21.60 yards per catch.

1415 A: Chuck Malito gained 166 yards against Hawaii in 1976.

1416 A: Troy Browhawn

1417 A: Calvin Jones had 298 yards against Kansas in 1991.

1418 A: 90 yards against Oklahoma State in 1992

1419 Q: What is the record for most men's basketball games won in a single season at Nebraska?

1420 Q: Whose career record of 81 pass receptions did Johnny Rodgers break?

1421 Q: What is the longest field goal in Nebraska football history?

1422 Q: What pitcher had 36 appearances for the Nebraska baseball team in 1994 to set an all-time Husker record?

1423 Q: Which Nebraska place kicker had a string of 83 consecutive PAT's without a miss?

1424 Q: What was the longest kickoff return in Nebraska football history?

1425 Q: Which Husker place kicker had the most consecutive field goals?

1426 Q: In what year did the Husker men's basketball team set the school record for most wins in a single season?

1427 Q: Which Husker gained the most kickoff return yards in his career?

1428 Q: Which Husker baseball player has the career school record with 48 home runs?

1429 Q: Which place kicker had the most field goals in Nebraska history?

1430 Q: What place kicker had the highest PAT conversions percentage in Nebraska history?

1431 Q: When did the Huskers play in their first Big Eight post-season basketball title game in the history of the school?

1432 Q: Which Nebraska place kicker had the most field goals in a single season?

1419 A: 26

1420 A: Jeff Kinney

1421 A: 55 yards by three kickers

1422 A: Mike Bellows

1423 A: Gregg Barrios

1424 A: In 1911 Owen Frank ran back a kickoff for 105 yards.

1425 A: Dale Klein had 9 consecutive field goals in 1985.

1426 A: 1991

1427 A: Tyrone Hughes gained 1443 yards.

1428 A: Bobby Benjamin

1429 A: Dale Klein kicked 27 field goals in his career.

1430 A: Kevin Seibel converted on 43 of 44 tries for a percentage of .977.

1431 A: 1991

1432 A: Gregg Barrios had 14 field goals in 1990.

1433 Q: Who is Nebraska's all-time leading kicker in terms of scoring?

1434 Q: With an amazing .451 batting average, which NU player tops the record books in slugging percentage?

1435 Q: What was the most points scored by a Nebraska football team in Memorial Stadium?

1436 Q: What was the longest run by an offensive lineman that resulted in a Husker touchdown?

1437 Q: What is the highest scoring shutout in Nebraska football history?

1438 Q: What is the most pass attempts made by a Nebraska team in a single game?

1439 Q: What is the school record for most hits in a single baseball game for the Huskers?

1440 Q: Name 1 of the 3 Huskers who scored the most touchdowns in a single game.

1441 Q: What is the school record for the fewest turnovers in a single season for an NU football team?

1442 Q: Who was the first Husker athlete to be a professional in one sport and compete for the Huskers in another?

1443 Q: Against what football team did the Huskers record an incredible 883 yards in total offense?

1444 Q: In what year did the Huskers average the most passing yards per game?

1445 Q: How many innings did Colorado and Nebraska play when their game set the NCAA record for the longest collegiate baseball game in history?

1446 Q: Who are the only Huskers to gain more than 2000 all-purpose yards in a single season ?

1433 A: Gregg Barrios scored 205 points during his Husker career.

1434 A: Marc Sagmoen

1435 A: 72 points against Iowa State in 1983

1436 A: Dean Steinkuhler ran a 19 yard Fumbleroosky play against Miami in the 1984 Orange Bowl.

1437 A: NU defeated the Haskell Indians 119-0 in 1910.

1438 A: 42 attempts against Iowa State in 1972

1439 A: 25 against UNLV in 1985

1440 A: Three players have scored 6: Bill Chaloupka in 1907, Harvey Rathbone in 1910 and Calvin Jones in 1991.

1441 A: 12 in 1992

1442 A: Erick Strickland

1443 A: New Mexico State in 1982

1444 A: Behind the arm of quarterback Dave Humm in 1972

1445 A: 22

1446 A: Johnny Rodgers and Mike Rozier

1447 Q: Which NU quarterback holds the freshman record for total offense in a single season?

1448 Q: What team did the Huskers first defeat in Buck Beltzer Stadium?

1449 Q: Which NU football player set the freshman season scoring record?

1450 Q: What is the largest combined score in a Nebraska football game?

1451 Q: Who is the current NU volleyball player that holds the #1 and #2 spots in kills per game for a single season?

1452 Q: What is the most points a NU football team has scored against a Big Eight opponent?

1453 Q: The 1983 NU football team set an NCAA record for touchdowns scored in a single season. How many TD's did they score: 76, 84, 87 or 95?

1454 Q: What is the NU team record for most interceptions in a single game?

1455 Q: What NU men's gymnast holds the school record for Floor Exercise and Horizontal Bar?

1456 Q: What was the longest scoring run by a defensive lineman in NU history?

1457 Q: In what year was the greatest number of points scored against the Husker football team in a single season?

1458 Q: Which Husker set an NU record in 1970 for most tackles in his career?

1459 Q: What NU men's gymnast won five individual Big Eight titles in 1964?

1460 Q: Which Husker had the most blocked punts in a single season?

1447 A: Turner Gill with 979 yards in 1980

1448 A: Kansas

1449 A: Will Curtis scored 48 points in 1981.

1450 A: A 102-31 victory over Creighton University in 1905

1451 A: Allison Weston

1452 A: 72 points against Iowa State in 1983

1453 A: 84 touchdowns

1454 A: Seven against Kansas State in 1970

1455 A: Scott Johnson

1456 A: In 1959 Leroy Zentic ran back a fumble 36 yards for a touchdown.

1457 A: The 1948 team gave up 273 points to 10 teams.

1458 A: Jerry Murtaugh

1459 A: Dennis Albers

1460 A: Wayne Meylan blocked 3 punts in 1966.

1461 Q: What is the most shutouts for a Nebraska football team in a single season?

1462 Q: What team was the Huskers' first shut-out victim in Buck Beltzer Stadium?

1463 Q: What famous running back scored on the longest touchdown run against a Nebraska football team?

1464 Q: Which Husker defender had the most interception yards in his career?

1465 Q: What NCAA record did the University of Nebraska set in 1981 during the men's gymnastics championships?

1466 Q: Which Nebraska player owns the record for most fumble recoveries in a single season?

1467 Q: Which Husker had the most total tackles in a single season?

1468 Q: Which NU defender made the most pass interceptions in a single season?

1469 Q: Which Husker had the most assisted tackles in his Nebraska football career?

1470 Q: How many Husker male gymnasts have won the Nissen Award?

1471 Q: In what season did the Huskers defense allow a school record 67.5 yards of rushing per game?

1472 Q: Which NU defender had the longest interception for a touchdown?

1473 Q: In what year was there a triple play for the first time in Buck Beltzer Stadium?

1474 Q: Which Nebraska defender had the most pass interceptions in his career?

1461 A: The 1902 Huskers recorded 10 straight shutouts.

1462 A: Kansas

1463 A: Gale Sayers of Kansas University

1464 A: Bill Kosch had 10 interceptions for 233 yards.

1465 A: An NCAA attendance record

1466 A: Broderick Thomas recovered 6 in 1986.

1467 A: Lee Kunz had 141 tackles in 1977.

1468 A: Three Huskers are tied for this record. Larry Wachholtz, Dana Stephenson and Bill Kosch each had 7 interceptions.

1469 A: Jerry Murtaugh

1470 A: Three: Jim Hartung, Wes Sutter and Tom Schlesinger

1471 A: 1967

1472 A: Willie Greenfield had a 95 yard interception to score in 1971.

1473 A: 1989

1474 A: Dana Stephenson with 14

1475 Q: What was the record of the first NU men's basketball team in the two-game season of 1896-97?

1476 Q: In which year did Nebraska have the most players chosen in an NFL draft?

1477 Q: What Nebraska athlete holds the record for the most letters won in his collegiate career?

1478 Q: Which Husker had the longest punt return in a bowl game?

1479 Q: Who owns the Husker men's gymnastics record on the pommel horse?

1480 Q: Which Husker owns a school record for the longest field goal in a bowl game?

1481 Q: What is the record for most wins in a season for the men's basketball program at Nebraska?

1482 Q: In the 1995 Orange Bowl, NU set an NCAA record for consecutive bowl appearances. How many did it take to set this record?

1483 Q: Within 1,000 people, what was the largest crowd at Memorial Stadium for a non- Big Eight opponent?

1484 Q: Which Husker gymnast holds the men's floor exercise record at Nebraska?

1485 Q: What was Nebraska's longest football winning streak?

1486 Q: Which university has played the Nebraska football team the most times?

1487 Q: Name the two Big Eight basketball programs that have a winning record against NU in the Devaney Center.

1488 Q: What is Nebraska's longest unbeaten streak in football?

1475 A: 2-0

1476 A: In 1975 Nebraska had 12 players chosen.

1477 A: Elmer Dohrmann lettered 11 times in four sports at Nebraska.

1478 A: Johnny Rodgers returned a 77 yard punt in the 1972 Orange Bowl.

1479 A: Jim Hartung

1480 A: Paul Rogers kicked a 50 yard field goal against Georgia in the 1969 Sun Bowl.

1481 A: 26 games won in the 1990-91 season

1482 A: 26 consecutive bowl games

1483 A: 76,510 people in 1983 filled the stadium to watch NU defeat UCLA.

1484 A: Scott Johnson

1485 A: The Huskers won 27 games between 1901 and 1904.

1486 A: Kansas

1487 A: Missouri and Oklahoma

1488 A: 34 games between 1912-1916

1489 Q: What is the longest losing streak in Husker football history?

1490 Q: During which season did Nebraska football establish a home game attendance record?

1491 Q: Who owns the scoring record for a single game in the Phillips 66 Big Eight Basketball Tournament?

1492 Q: For which NCAA scoring record did Nebraska and Colorado combine efforts?

1493 Q: Which Husker gymnast holds the men's still rings school record?

1494 Q: Nebraska expanded the strength complex in the West Stadium in 1989. How many square feet does this strength facility cover?

1495 Q: What was the greatest combined score in a Nebraska Big Eight football game?

1496 Q: Which Husker gymnast holds the men's vault record at NU?

1497 Q: How many times has an NU football team shut-out every opponent they faced during a season?

1498 Q: Who holds an unofficial record for breaking an average of two helmets a year in his NU football career?

1499 Q: Which NU basketball athlete holds the school record in field goal percentage?

1500 Q: What was NU's record the year before Bob Devaney arrived?

1501 Q: Which Husker gymnast holds the men's parallel bars record at Nebraska?

1502 Q: What is the Husker's winning percentage in Memorial Stadium through the 1994 season: .650, .725, 740 or .800?

1489 A: Seven games, occurring in the 1957 season

1490 A: 1988 with an average of 76,342 fans

1491 A: NU's Eric Piatkowski with 42 points

1492 A: They combined for 41 points in 2 minutes and 55 seconds on the scoreboard clock.

1493 A: Jim Hartung

1494 A: 30,000 square feet (making it the largest on a college campus)

1495 A: 101 points with Iowa State in 1983

1496 A: Chris Riegel

1497 A: Two times: 1890 and 1902

1498 A: Mike Knox who played linebacker from 1981-85

1499 A: Dave Hoppen

1500 A: Three wins, six losses and one tie

1501 A: Kevin Davis

1502 A: .740

1503 Q: Which team won the first NU - Iowa football game?

1504 Q: Name the two NU men's basketball players who share the record for most minutes played in a single game?

1505 Q: Which team broke Bob Devaney's 33 game win streak?

1506 Q: What was NU's biggest losing margin in the history of Memorial Stadium?

1507 Q: Which Husker gymnast holds the men's horizontal bar record at Nebraska?

1508 Q: Which NU offensive lineman established the squat record at 650 pounds in 1982?

1509 Q: Who is the fastest lineman in the history of Nebraska football?

1510 Q: What event holds the attendance record at the Bob Devaney Sports Center?

1511 Q: What was Bob Devaney's bowl record in his tenure as Husker coach?

1512 Q: Which Big Eight school has won the most conference football championships?

1513 Q: Nebraska's 1974 Sugar Bowl victory tied what national bowl record?

1514 Q: In what year did the men's basketball team lose the most games?

1515 Q: How many consecutive wins did Nebraska have prior to the 1984 Orange Bowl loss?

1516 Q: His 230 yards passing in the 1966 Orange Bowl stands as a Nebraska record. Name him.

1517 Q: Which Husker male swimmer holds the 50 Freestyle record at NU?

1503 A: Iowa

1504 A: Jack Moore and Andre Smith each played 60 minutes.

1505 A: UCLA

1506 A: 54 points in a 1945 loss to Minnesota

1507 A: Scott Johnson

1508 A: Dave Rimington

1509 A: Neil Smith with a (4.63) 40 yard dash

1510 A: The 1978 John Denver concert

1511 A: 6 wins and 3 losses

1512 A: Nebraska

1513 A: Most consecutive bowl game victories

1514 A: 19 games in 1963

1515 A: Twenty-two

1516 A: Bob Churchich

1517 A: Peter Williams

1518 Q: What is the NU record for most points scored in a bowl game?

1519 Q: The 1980 Cotton Bowl game marked what "first" for the weight training program?

1520 Q: What was the score of NU's first basketball game in 1897?

1521 Q: What weight lifting record did I.M. Hipp break in 1976?

1522 Q: Within 1 inch, what was Allen Lyday's vertical jump record from 1982?

1523 Q: Which Husker male swimmer holds the 100 Freestyle record at Nebraska?

1524 Q: When did the football team drop the stripes from the sleeves of their uniforms?

1525 Q: Which Husker quarterback rushed for the most touchdowns in a single game?

1526 Q: How many games did the NU men's basketball team play in its first season?

1527 Q: Who was the player that had the longest scoring and non-scoring runs in the 1974 season?

1528 Q: Which Husker male swimmer holds the 200 and 400 individual medley records at NU?

1529 Q: Which Nebraska back holds the school record for the highest average gain per carry in a single season?

1530 Q: Which NU back had the longest scoring and non-scoring runs of the 1978 football season?

1531 Q: Whose Big Eight career rushing record was broken by Mike Rozier in 1983?

1532 Q: When was the first winning season for the Huskers men's basketball team?

1518 A: 45 in the 1969 Sun Bowl

1519 A: It was the first time a college team took a portable weight room to a bowl game.

1520 A: NU-11, Lincoln YMCA-8

1521 A: A record hip-sled lift of 915 pounds

1522 A: 39.5 inches

1523 A: Allen Kelsey

1524 A: 1977

1525 A: Gerry Gdowski rushed for four in 1989.

1526 A: Two

1527 A: Monte Anthony

1528 A: Jan Bidrman

1529 A: Mike Rozier averaged 7.81 yards per carry in 1983.

1530 A: Rick Berns

1531 A: Terry Miller (Oklahoma State)

1532 A: The first season in 1897

1533 Q: Which NU fullback scored the most rushing touchdowns in his career?

1534 Q: Whose NCAA record was broken by Mike Rozier when he rushed for 929 yards in four games?

1535 Q: Which NU football player had the longest scoring and non-scoring runs during the 1977 season?

1536 Q: When was the first losing season for the Huskers men's basketball program?

1537 Q: Which Husker had the longest scoring and non-scoring runs in the 1970 season?

1538 Q: Mike Rozier broke which Big Eight running back's NCAA record for highest gain per rush in a career?

1539 Q: In which game did Rick Berns break the existing single game rushing record in 1978?

1540 Q: Which Husker back recorded 36 rushing attempts in a single game to establish a new school record?

1541 Q: In what year did the NU men's basketball team produce its first All- American player?

1542 Q: What NCAA record did tight end Gerald Armstrong tie in 1992?

1543 Q: Which Husker tight end holds the school record for most pass receptions in a career for that position?

1544 Q: Which Husker male swimmer was the first to earn All-American status?

1545 Q: What was the first season for a Nebraska receiver to have 3 touchdown catches in a single game?

1546 Q: Which Husker kicker had the best field goal success by percentage in his career?

1533 A: Mark Schellen

1534 A: Marcus Allen

1535 A: I.M. Hipp

1536 A: 1898; the second season

1537 A: Joe Orduna

1538 A: Billy Sims

1539 A: Missouri

1540 A: Rick Berns in 1978

1541 A: 1913

1542 A: Armstrong was 6-for-6, all for touchdowns before catching a ball that did not produce a score.

1543 A: Jerry List

1544 A: Pete Heglein in 1945

1545 A: Clarence Swanson did it in 1921.

1546 A: Dean Sukup

1547 Q: Against which Big Eight team did Gerry Gdowski score four touchdowns rushing to set a school record?

1548 Q: Which Husker kicker missed only 2 PAT's in his career to set a school record in 1990?

1549 Q: What is the longest punt return in Nebraska school history?

1550 Q: Which Husker ran the fastest 100-meter dash in NU history?

1551 Q: What is the record for points scored in the first quarter of a Husker football game?

1552 Q: Which NU football player finished his career by producing the most total yards of offense: Johnny Rodgers or Jerry Tagge?

1553 Q: Who was the first All-American men's basketball player for NU?

1554 Q: What is Nebraska's football record for consecutive games being shut-out?

1555 Q: Against which Big Eight team in 1972 did NU establish its all-time single game passing record?

1556 Q: Which Husker was responsible for the fastest 50-yard dash run indoors at Nebraska?

1557 Q: In which season did NU allow the fewest number of points: 1890 or 1902?

1558 Q: With how many points per game did Carl Underwood lead the Missouri Valley con ference in scoring in 1913: 6.6, 8.5 or 12?

1559 Q: What is the greatest amount of points NU has given up in a single quarter of a football game: 21, 28, 30 or 35?

1547 A: Iowa State in 1989

1548 A: Gregg Barrios

1549 A: 92 yards

1550 A: Riley Washington

1551 A: 35 against OSU in 1988

1552 A: Jerry Tagge

1553 A: Sam Carrier

1554 A: 4 games between the 1942-43 seasons

1555 A: Kansas

1556 A: Charlie Greene

1557 A: In both years NU shut out all opponents.

1558 A: 6.6 points

1559 A: 28 against UCLA in 1988

1560 Q: In which year did the Husker football team have the best turnover margin: 1902, 1960, 1971 or 1983?

1561 Q: In which season did NU give up the fewest passing yards: 1950, 1973 or 1994?

1562 Q: In which year did Nebraska give up the fewest rushing yards: 1967, 1974 or 1993?

1563 Q: What record do Joe Blahak, Ric Lindquist and Dana Stephenson have in common as NU defensive backs?

1564 Q: What was the seating capacity of the Coliseum when it was built in 1926?

1565 Q: Which NU defender had the most assisted tackles in a season: Jerry Murtaugh, Lee Kunz or John Dutton?

1566 Q: Which Husker holds the all-time school record in the men's high jump?

1567 Q: Which NU defender had the longest interception return without scoring: Joe Blahak, Bret Clark or Ric Lindquist?

1568 Q: Which team prevented the Huskers from setting an NCAA consecutive bowl victory record?

1569 Q: In what season did the Nebraska men's basketball team earn its first NCAA playoff appearance?

1570 Q: What was the longest pass reception by a Husker in a bowl game: 56, 71 or 99 yards?

1571 Q: Nebraska only produced how many first downs against Colorado in 1961: 0, 4, 9 or 12?

1572 Q: Which Husker holds the all-time school record in the men's long jump?

1573 Q: What was the largest winning margin for the Huskers against a Big Eight opponent in Memorial Stadium?

1560 A: 1971, of course

1561 A: 1973

1562 A: 1967

1563 A: The most intercepted passes in a single game

1564 A: 8,000

1565 A: Lee Kunz

1566 A: Darren Burton

1567 A: Bret Clark

1568 A: Arizona State in 1975

1569 A: 1948-49

1570 A: 56 yards in the 1972 Orange Bowl

1571 A: "0," If you can believe it

1572 A: Robert Thomas

1573 A: NU beat Missouri 62-0 in 1972

1574 Q: What is the longest Big Eight win streak for the Huskers in Memorial Stadium: 9, 12, 15 or 22?

1575 Q: What year was the last season for the Big Seven conference to have a three-way champion in men's basketball?

1576 Q: In what year was the largest margin of victory enjoyed by the Huskers over the Oklahoma Sooners under Bob Devaney?

1577 Q: How many lead changes were there in the 1971 Game of the Century: 0, 2, 4, or 7?

1578 Q: What was the first game Nebraska lost after winning the 1971 national championship?

1579 Q: In what year was the Husker football team first ranked in the final UPI poll?

1580 Q: Who was the first Husker men's basketball player to be selected to the East-West All-Star game?

1581 Q: What was Nebraska's longest winning streak in Memorial Stadium?

1582 Q: When was the last time that Nebraska lost a homecoming game?

1583 Q: How long was NU football's unbeaten streak from 1969 to 1972?

1584 Q: What was the last team to forfeit a game against the Nebraska football team?

1585 Q: How many school records did Bus Whitehead have when he graduated from Nebraska: 3, 5, 9 or 12?

1586 Q: How many losing seasons did NU football have in the first 50 seasons: 2, 9 or 15?

1587 Q: At what non-bowl game did the Husker football team play in front of the largest crowd?

1574 A: 15

1575 A: 1950

1576 A: 1969 (NU-44, OU-14)

1577 A: 4

1578 A: The Huskers lost the 1972 opener to UCLA.

1579 A: 1963

1580 A: Milton "Bus" Whitehead

1581 A: NU won 23 straight games between 1969-72.

1582 A: A shutout by Kansas State in 1968

1583 A: 33 games

1584 A: Kansas State in 1951

1585 A: Nine

1586 A: Only 2

1587 A: At Penn State in 1982

1588 Q: When were the Huskers last shut out in Memorial Stadium?

1589 Q: Who was the first Cornhusker to score 1000 points in his career for the NU basketball team?

1590 Q: Who was Nebraska's first athletic director?

1588 A: Kansas State in 1968

1589 A: Herschell Turner

1590 A: William "Bill" Orwig

1508 Q: Which NU offensive lineman established the squat record at 650 pounds in 1982?

The Voice of the Nebraska Cornhuskers

Kent Pavelka delivers all of the play-by-play action for KFAB and its 50 station radio network. Kent begins his twelfth consecutive season of play-by-play and his 22nd season covering Nebraska football on KFAB.

Also included in this all-star broadcast lineup is veteran color commentator Gary Sadlemyer as well as "Husker Huddle" and "Sports Day Mid America" host Jim Rose.

Pavelka also delivers all the basketball action. Color commentary is delivered by Nebraska Sports Information Assistant, Nick Joos and by KMTV's Sportscaster, Rich Roberts.

The talent of the KFAB Football/Basketball broadcast team truly is the sound and excitement that makes Cornhusker Sports coverage on KFAB a winning combination.

Nebraska Licensing Program

Under the direction of Chris Bahl, Licensing Director, the University of Nebraska is maximizing its revenue potential to the benefit of the athletic department and the licensee merchandisers.

Chris did his undergraduate work at Kansas State University earning a bachelor's degree in Political Science/Public Administration. He served as a graduate assistant in the Athletic Department of both Wichita State University and the Unversity of Nebraska. Chris went on to graduate from Wichita State with a master's degree in Sports Administration. Prior to taking charge of the licensing program, Chris worked in the Athletic Marketing Office handling marketing and promotions of special events and projects.

The 1994-95 fiscal year was the finest ever in the history of the University of Nebraska. Working closely with our exclusive licensing agent, the Collegiate Licensing Company (CLC), the royalty rate increased from 7.5% to 12% for national championship related merchandise and the number of new licensees was limited. Nebraska ranks 5th among the 150+ CLC member institutions with over 2.1 million dollar of royalties collected on the sale of over $58,000,000 in retail sales of officially licensed UN merchandise. These astonishing figures represent an increase over the previous year of 372%!

University of Nebraska Sports Information Office

The goal of the Nebraska Sports Information Director's office is to effectively communicate to the news media, to the general public and to other interested groups, information about our athletic programs in order to positively promote all 22 varsity individual teams and its athletes. Each sport publication is written to appeal to media, to fans, and to future Huskers.

The Nebraska SID office produces media guides, posters, schedule cards, game-day programs and news releases for each of the University's varsity sports. The office is also responsible for responding to news media inquires; arranging all players and coach interviews; providing game-day management and statistical services; serving as a historian in terms of results, photo, film and newspaper clip files; serve as a liaison to various athletic governing bodies such as NCAA, the Big Eight Conference and to other sanctioned offices; and serves as a liaison to the general public in order to increase public support and knowledge of each Husker sport and sporting events.

Last year, the SID office wrote, designed and edited 16 media/recruiting guides. All the printed materials are produced on a computer desktop publishing system in the SID office and printed on campus. The Sports Information Office sells both posters and media/recruiting guides to the general public to help cover the printing and distribution/mailing costs.

Working closely with the Academic office, another SID focus is to ensure individual Huskers earn academic achievement recognition.

The SID office is a busy, proud, professional, and vital part of the sports programs at the University of Nebraska.

Nebraska Bookstore began in 1915 as a retail bookstore. Originally known as Long's Bookstore, the business operated successfully as a textbook store through 1934, when it was sold to Johnny Johnson and became Nebraska Bookstore. Under the direction of Mr. Johnson the store began to change. Although textbooks remained the central commodity, paperback books and basic school supplies began to appear on the shelves during the late 1950s and 1960s. Clothing entered the scene in the mid 1960s and early 1970s. In late 1973 Johnny Johnson sold the business to Lincoln Industries incorporated.

Nebraska Bookstore was then located across from the University of Nebraska - Lincoln at 1135 'R' Street. When It was purchased in 1973, the University's 20 year plan called for the annexation of the store's property. Although a move was being planned, the construction of the Leid Center called for relocation sooner than anticipated. The new Nebraska Bookstore, completed in 1986, is very different from the old store. Nebraska Bookstore is now the largest retail business in downtown Lincoln.

Nebraska Bookstore's products and services have changed over time. What started out as a textbook outlet for the students has become a dynamic, multi-department, service oriented business with over 100 employees. The early staff worked in a clerk-service situation where they took individual student textbook requests and retrieved them for the customer. Today's staff performs a variety of functions for numerous services in the ever changing retail department/book store.

Today, Nebraska Bookstore features 14 departments including a book department with over 150,000 titles in stock, CD ROM Shop/Multi Media, textbooks, electronics, gifts, emblematic Big Red Collection, supplies, sundries, periodicals, art and engineering supplies, copy center, desktop publishing, custom framing and a full service U.S. Post Office substation.

custom framing and a full service U.S. Post Office substation.

Through serving the University of Nebraska - Lincoln students, faculty and staff, Lincoln, Nebraska, the Nation and beyond, Nebraska Bookstore is continuously striving to meet the needs of customers and proud of the quality products and services it provides.